Hack-Proof Your Life Now!

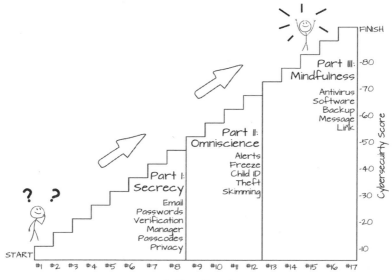

HACK-PROOF YOUR LIFE NOW!

THE NEW CYBERSECURITY RULES:
Protect your email, computers, and bank accounts from hacks, malware, and identity theft

SEAN M. BAILEY and DEVIN KROPP

New York

Publisher's Cataloging-In-Publication Data
Names: Bailey, Sean M., 1959- | Kropp, Devin.
Title: Hack-proof your life now! : the new cybersecurity rules : protect your email, computers, and bank accounts from hacks, malware, and identity theft / Sean M. Bailey and Devin Kropp.
Other Titles: Hack proof your life now!
Description: First edition. | New York : Horsesmouth, [2016] | Includes bibliographical references and index.
Identifiers: LCCN 2016910097 | ISBN 978-0-9977290-0-9 (softcover) | ISBN 978-0-9977290-1-6 (ebook)
Subjects: LCSH: Computer security. | Computer crimes--Prevention. | Identity theft--Prevention. | Malware (Computer software) | Finance, Personal.
Classification: LCC QA76.9.A25 B35 2016 (print) | LCC QA76.9.A25 (ebook) | DDC 005.8--dc23

Ordering Information
Special discounts are available on quantity purchases by corporations, associations, and other organizations. For information contact:

Horsesmouth, LLC
888-336-6884 (Outside the U.S.: 212-343-8760)
books@horsesmouth.com
21 West 38th Street
New York, NY 10018
Horsesmouth.com
Printed in the United States of America

10 9 8 7 6 5 4 3 2 1

Jacket design by Steve Pazenski.
Cover and interior illustrations by Marissa Bernstel

For the two women who bring out the very best in me: Nancy, my wife, partner, and beautiful love, and Charlotte, our daughter, whose courage, empathy, and exuberance for life always leave me in awe.

– SMB

For my parents, whose love, strength, and support allowed me to follow my dreams.

– DK

Contents

Part III: Mindfulness

Hack-Proof Action Guide

Introduction

Click.

A finger tap is the most common and necessary action we take on our computers and devices. It's also the most dangerous, as my colleagues and I experienced one day in our Manhattan offices: We watched an extortion plot unfold right under our noses, and the hack started with a simple click. It always does.

Our firm teaches financial planners to educate the public about personal finance topics. Ever since the 2013 hack of the discount retailer Target, we had become sensitized to the growing cases of cyber thieves stealing people's credit-card numbers and personal information. When we talked to our friends and colleagues about their cybersecurity knowledge and their own misadventures with hackers, we realized people needed comprehensive guidance on how to avoid becoming a cyber victim. The Target breach spurred us to act, and we made it our mission to create a jargon-free personal cybersecurity program that could be learned quickly and used easily.

Now we faced a dangerous spam attack right inside our network. Our company takes security seriously. We have a full-time tech team, with state-of-the-art defenses deployed throughout our computer networks. In fifteen years, we'd never encountered any serious cybersecurity trouble until this moment.

Everyone in our company received the same fake email from the electronic fax company eFax, and the spam message contained a link to Dropbox. An alert staff member launched a warning to everyone: "Don't open that email! Delete it immediately!"

But it was too late.

One of us asked a nearby colleague, "Did you see that eFax spam?" An odd look fell over his face, a combination of confusion, shame, and horror. He'd just clicked the link. And in that moment, our coworker joined the ranks of an estimated eighty-eight thousand daily victims of "phishing attacks,"[1] a hacker ploy often included in billions of spam messages sent each day.[2]

By clicking that phishing link to Dropbox, he had downloaded a malicious software (malware) program called CryptoWall 2.0, which immediately started its extortion. The background on his computer turned blue and then a white page appeared on his screen announcing: "Your files are encrypted. To get the key to decrypt files you have to pay 500USD/EUR."

The hackers had kidnapped our colleague's computer. And they turned up the pressure immediately: Pay the extortion price of $500 within forty-eight hours or the ransom would double.

Our coworker is a smart person—knowledgeable, attentive, and skilled at his job. He had actively participated in our internal discussions about cybersecurity. He had never received an eFax email or used the Internet storage service Dropbox. He didn't know the sender, but without thinking first, he clicked a link and stumbled into a cyber shakedown scheme known as ransomware—and in that one instant he gave control of his computer and all its files to a cyber thief.

Even worse, the malware program hopped from his computer to our office's central network—just sitting there, a file with an innocuous-sounding name waiting to be clicked again so it could spread and repeat its attack.

Fortunately, we didn't need to pay the ransom. Our IT staff restored the computer from a backup file. However, our associate lost two months of data.

We offer this story as a small warning. We don't want you to suffer the way our colleague and many others do every day. Cybersecurity is a serious personal issue, and we all need to know how to protect ourselves. Let us teach you how.

How to Use This Book to Boost Your Cybersecurity

We want to give you a simple, effective, and realistic framework for boosting your cybersecurity—one that you can achieve quickly.

We define cybersecurity as the personal behaviors and actions you take to protect yourself in the online world from identity theft, frauds, and other crimes aimed at stealing your personal information and data.

We've scoured the entire cybersecurity world, researching the practices of both security experts and ordinary Internet users like ourselves. Our recommendations cover the biggest threats you and your family face, and show you the best methods for protecting your identity and personal data. You just need to learn and implement the New Cybersecurity Rules that we'll explain in the following pages.

We've organized this book around three critical mindsets of your cyber life that we describe as Secrecy, Omniscience, and Mindfulness. Each of these sections includes an explanation of why that theme is important. We then introduce you to a series of rules that relate to each mindset. We start every chapter with a "Hack Report," a story we've pulled from our research files that shows how someone's poor cybersecurity led to serious problems. Then we give you a rule to follow and direction on how to close that cybersecurity vulnerability.

Nearly every chapter closes with a "Hack-Proof Action Step." Each one you take raises your knowledge and boosts your cybersecurity.

Once you've completed an action, mark your progress at the chapter end or use the checklist starting on page 128. (Our Hack-Proof Action Guide that begins on page 133 will answer your questions about implementing any rule.)

None of our recommendations will take long or cost much money. What they will do is thwart the hackers, frustrate the spammers, and shut the door on identity thieves. By the end of the book, we guarantee you will be prepared to protect yourself and your family from the cyber crime wave targeting us. All we require of you is an open mind to changing your cybersecurity attitude and taking action. In so doing, you will learn to hack-proof your life. The first step begins by discovering your personal Cybersecurity Score.

Cybersecurity Knowledge Gap

In a moment, we're going to ask you to take a quick self-assessment so you learn your current Cybersecurity Score, an actual measure of your knowledge. Once you know your vulnerabilities, we think you'll be more open to taking actions that boost your security.

Hacking bedevils everyone in society right up to the highest levels of business and government. Indeed, the authors of *Cybersecurity and Cyberwar*, P. W. Singer and Allan Friedman, contend that a cyber world war is under way, and we're all involved. The authors contend that our biggest problem is that we face a "Cybersecurity Knowledge Gap," a new development in recent years. Back in the late 1990s and early 2000s, most hackers were amateurs, and we largely faced malicious computer attacks carried out for sport or notoriety, though some were criminal. Today we face a range of motives: criminal activity, espionage, terrorism, and warfare. The hackers often represent criminal gangs and even belligerent governments.[3]

So, cybersecurity is not just a personal issue, it also concerns our business life, and even the protection and safety of nations. The U.S. government now considers cyber attacks a national security threat;

President Obama put cyber warfare under the Department of Defense's Strategic Command in 2009.[4] Congress has even directed the military to carry out simulated cyber "war games" against Russia, China, Iran, and North Korea.[5]

We all need advice and regular reminders about how to stay safe. The headlines confirm this nearly every day. But no one guides us on how to close our cybersecurity gap to become safe and stay safe online. That's why we want you to start by measuring your online security knowledge. We all know that improving our lives involves taking action, but we need to know where to start—and that applies to cybersecurity, too. Let's begin right now and determine your current Cybersecurity Score—it takes just two minutes.

Discover Your Cybersecurity Score

Circle your answers to the following statements, then follow the instructions below to get your score.

1. I have one email address that I use *exclusively* for my online financial accounts (banking, credit cards, payment services, brokerage, etc.) and nothing else.　　Yes　No

2. I have two-step login (two-factor authentication) turned on for my email and online financial accounts.　　Yes　No

3. I can spot the difference between dangerous *free* public Wi-Fi and useful, secure *free* public Wi-Fi.　　Yes　No

4. I understand how to tell if my home Wi-Fi   Yes   No
network is vulnerable to hackers and how to
boost the network's security.

5. Whenever any money leaves my bank accounts   Yes   No
or my credit cards are charged, I'm alerted to
the transaction.

6. I have complete control over my credit files at   Yes   No
the big-three bureaus (Equifax, Experian, and
TransUnion), because I have placed them on
the highest security level.

7. I have confirmed with the credit bureaus that   Yes   No
my minor children have not been the victims
of identity theft.

8. I run an updated antivirus software program   Yes   No
on my computers and devices.

9. I always make sure that my computer and   Yes   No
devices have the most up-to-date software
programs, including operating system, browsers,
Microsoft Office, iTunes player, virus protection,
wireless router, and Adobe's PDF reader.

10. I have a system for ensuring that I can recover   Yes   No
from a ransomware phishing attack without
paying an extortion fee to a criminal.

Your Cybersecurity Score

Give yourself five points for each Yes answer. Add up your points to discover your Cybersecurity Score. Don't worry about a low rating, because it will rise as you complete our recommended action steps and create your personal cybersecurity system. Let's get started!

Rating

50-40	GOOD
35–25	WEAK
20–0	DANGER

PART I

Secrecy

Increase Your Stealth, Boost Your Security

Regardless of anyone's Cybersecurity Score, we must accept and act upon the strong likelihood that hackers already compromised our personal security. The theft happened some time during the last few years, as the world witnessed an unprecedented wave of cyber attacks and data breaches.

Just consider this: Security experts estimate that fraudsters send upward of thirty-four trillion emails per year—ninety-four billion per day. Ninety percent of all spam carries malicious attachments or dangerous links aimed at stealing your money.[1] Some of those poisoned emails triggered break-ins of corporate and government computer systems that led to your birth date, Social Security number, employment history, residential addresses, and other identifying data falling into the hands of nefarious organizations.

We all know someone whose email account was hacked, credit card or bank account falsely used, or identity stolen. A few years ago, it was estimated that more than thirteen million people suffer from identity theft each year—that's one new victim every two seconds.[2] One study by *Consumer Reports* estimates that in recent years, cybercriminals stole the personal identifying information of more than seventy million Americans.[3] In 2016, the Identity Theft Resource Center estimated that nearly 170 million records were stolen the previous year.[4] The number of victims keeps growing and almost every adult has a connection to an organization penetrated by hackers in recent years.

Data Breach Victims

Here's a partial list of companies and organizations that have lost control over some or all of their customer data since 2005:

Adobe, TD Ameritrade, Anthem, AOL, AT&T, Bank of America, Bank of New York Mellon, Blue Cross/Blue Shield, P.F. Chang's, Card Systems, Chicago voter database, Citigroup, Community Health Systems, Countrywide Financial Corp., Dairy Queen, eBay, Evernote, Experian/ Court Ventures, Facebook, Fidelity National Information Services, Gawker, Global Payments, Inc., Goodwill, Hannaford Brothers, HealthNet, Heartland Payment Systems/Certegy Check Services Inc., Horizon Blue Cross Blue Shield of New Jersey, Home Depot, Honda, Hyatt Hotels, Internal Revenue Service, Jimmy John's, Kmart, LivingSocial, Ashley Madison, T.J. Maxx, MBIA Inc., Michael's, JPMorgan Chase, Nationwide Mutual Insurance Company and Allied Insurance, National Archive and Records Administration, Neiman Marcus, Office of Personnel Management, Office of the Texas Attorney General, Oklahoma Department of Human Services, Premera Blue Cross Blue Shield, RSA Security, Sally Beauty, Scottrade, Sony Corporation, South Carolina Department of Revenue, Target, T-Mobile, U.S. Department of Veterans Affairs, RBS Worldpay, Wyndham Hotels and Resorts, and Zappos.[5]

Staggering, isn't it? Yet the statistics don't count organizations (public and private) that were hacked but said nothing about it, or those organizations that have hackers prowling inside their networks right now and simply don't know it.

A New Level of Stealth Required

Stolen personal data can deliver big paydays for thieves who routinely buy and sell swiped information used to impersonate us in cyber frauds. Individually, the prices your personal details command seem small: For instance, hackers receive just two dollars for selling one Walmart login[6] and up to eight dollars for one iTunes login.[7] But when miscreants possess millions of credentials to sell, the value of the digital booty adds up: Experts estimate that swiped personal information translates into fraudulent activities valued at $16 billion a year.[8]

While you can't stop hackers from sweeping up your data held by corporations and governments, you *can* make it fruitless for criminals to use. More importantly, by adopting a new level of secrecy in a few critical aspects of your life—drawing a tighter security ring around your personal and financial data—you can boost your security and regain confidence that you'll be safe from most types of cyber fraud.

Once you learn the New Cybersecurity Rules and complete the action steps in this first section, you'll have a new approach to email, new security measures to block hackers, new ways to handle passwords, new methods to safely connect to the Internet at home and in public, plus clear directions on keeping your connected devices safe and enjoying social media without worry. Follow our recommendations and your Cybersecurity Score will improve as you start to hack-proof your life.

1

Your Email Address Is the Key to Your Digital Life: It Shouldn't Be Everywhere!

The Case of the Professor Who Hacked His Friend's Bank Account

HACK REPORT: Herbert Thompson, a software security expert and professor, wanted to show how easy it is to break into a person's online bank account. He decided to conduct an experiment and recruited his wife's friend as his target.

Writing in *Scientific American*, Thompson detailed the steps he took to unlock the woman's bank account.[1] He started with only her name, hometown, and employer. The professor knew that one little personal fact often provides a stepping stone that unravels someone's entire weak security system. So he Googled the woman's name and discovered two sources of information about her: an old résumé and a personal blog. Both would prove critical to Thompson's challenge—the blog contained the woman's personal email address and the résumé included her college email.

Pulling up the school's email login page first, he used the "reset password" feature to start the break-in. The system asked Thompson to answer a security question about the woman's birthday. He knew the answer, because she had discussed it on her blog. Voilà! Thompson had cracked her alumni email.

From there, Thompson could see a possible path to the woman's bank account. First, he needed to crack her personal email, so he went to that account's login page and started another reset password request, which sent an email to her secondary address—the college email account he now controlled.

Again he answered the account's challenge question with facts gleaned from the résumé and blog posts, breaking the security of her personal email address and changing its password. Now he was just one step from the woman's bank account, which used her personal email.

Once more Thompson used the reset password feature for her online banking and answered the security questions with details from her résumé and blog (pet name, phone number, college). That's all the professor needed. He cracked the account's security, changed its password, and had instant access to the money. Mission accomplished.

"Her whole digital identity sat precariously on the foundation of her college email account; once I had access to it, the rest of the security defenses fell like a row of dominoes," Thompson wrote. "For many of us, the abundance of personal information we put online combined with the popular model of sending a password reset email has our online security resting unsteadily on the shoulders of one or two email accounts."

Thompson's experiment demonstrated the many pitfalls and weaknesses we face with our cybersecurity. Our personal identifying information appears in many places on the Internet, and it's hard to hide or remove. Hackers can find it, too.

Rule #1: Create a Secret Email Address for Your Financial Accounts

Secrecy is an essential ingredient to a stronger, more secure digital life and something we all need more of in this age. Being more private, more discreet, indeed more secret is simply a must. And this secrecy starts with your email.

Let's look at what happens when a hacker tricks you into revealing enough of your personal data to seize your email account—or gains entry other ways. You must understand the danger before you learn our New Cybersecurity Rules about email and passwords.

For many of us, our primary email address, whether personal or business, unlocks the rest of our digital life. Once a cyber crook seizes any email account linked to other logins, such as online banking, he just needs to run a "reset password" request to start causing trouble. And getting hacked involves a wider violation than just the loss of money. As our communication choices have expanded from paper to computers to tablets and smartphones, we've all become digital citizens with vast amounts of our personal lives recorded on the Internet. While we think our username and password protect us, once a hacker pilfers our email credentials, he gains a commanding view over our lives. Let's look at what an email breach exposes.

Anatomy of an Email Hack

For starters, a break-in of your primary email account exposes your private life: your correspondences, names, addresses, phone numbers, appointments, emails, birth dates, and passwords, plus photos, videos, or other recordings. Suddenly, the hacker possesses a trove of your personal information.

From your email account, the cyber thief can see the places you conduct commerce on the web. Think of your accounts with companies such as Amazon, Apple, iTunes, FedEx, Google, eBay, Walmart, United Airlines, and hundreds more.

Any social media sites you frequent also become vulnerable, including your accounts at Facebook, Twitter, Instagram, and Pinterest. In addition, a hacker can view your online public life: organizations you support, donations you've made, and petitions you have signed.

The threats even bleed into your medical life. People communicate with their doctors (and insurance companies) by email and log in to "patient portals" to review tests and discuss medications, treatments, and payments. The wider use of electronic medical records (EMR) only heightens the danger of an email hack.

Your inbox also may reflect your business life. It contains your contacts, company documents, meeting notes, client notes, competitive intelligence, expense reports, employee reviews, salary records, business plans, and other sensitive files.

The same is true about your community life. If you sit on a committee or board of a local nonprofit, hackers can access sensitive documents including capital plans, donor lists, fundraising strategies, volunteer problems, board politics, staff issues, and communication with executive staff.

Email Address Vulnerability

Finally, and most importantly, your email account opens the door to your financial life: checking and savings, debit, direct deposit, credit card, PayPal, and other services. Quickly the hacker who invades your email account and resets your password exercises vast control over your digital life. Shocked barely conveys the violation when you view your loss of privacy through the lens of an email hack. Now you can understand why security experts say that when a hacker owns your email, he owns your life, at least on the Internet.[2] Stopping that from ever happening requires a mindset of Secrecy—a key element to stronger cybersecurity.

We don't think twice about sharing our email address with countless businesses, organizations, and people. If you've used the Internet for any amount of time, you have entered your address at dozens of online accounts for shopping, traveling, exercising, gaming, dating, and hundreds of other activities. But having your email addresses in so many *hacked* databases puts you at a significant risk. Our stolen personal data, paired with questionable security, puts the criminals in position to seize our email, break into other accounts linked to that address, and inflict mayhem.[3]

Reduce Your Digital Footprint

We need to protect our most important accounts from this fate. You may not care if someone hacks your Food Network account, but you don't want your online banking exposed in the same way. Using the same email address for each is not a safe practice.

Reduce your digital footprint by creating a secret email address for your financial accounts.[4] You want to eliminate the chance that the email address you've used for dozens of websites—including banking—gets scooped up in the next gigantic data breach.

Make sure your secret email address reveals nothing about you: Do not incorporate your first name, last name, initials, or other identifying personal information in your username. When selecting your password reset option, choose the most secure option available. Many email providers have started phasing out password recovery questions because the answers can often be found by searching on the Internet. Instead, many offer recovery phone numbers or recovery email addresses. When you need to reset your password, a code or link will be sent to you. Pick the more secure phone number reset option, since it would require the hacker to have access to your device to complete the break-in. You just don't want your everyday email linked to your secret financial email address. By keeping them separate, you're maintaining secrecy and increasing the likelihood that hackers never enter your bank account.

Hack-Proof Action Step #1

☐ Create a secret email address for your financial accounts and set it up with the strongest possible security settings.

Completion date: __/__/____   Score: 5 points

For recommendations on setting up your financial-only email address, turn to page 136 of the Action Guide in the back of the book.

2

Love Your Passwords, Lose Weight, and Beat the Password Paradox

Better Living Through Meaningful Passwords

HACK REPORT: Even life's most stressful and anguishing events can produce positive outcomes. Consider the story of creative director Mauricio Estrella. Following a difficult divorce, he developed a healthier, more positive outlook—no more sweating the small stuff at work, such as having to create a new password every thirty days as required by his IT department. To lessen that annoyance, Estrella had a brilliant idea. He would make his new password a personal goal.

His first one was about forgiving his ex-wife: Forgive@h3r. "That simple action changed the way I looked at my ex-wife," Estrella wrote in a column on the website *Medium*.[1] "That constant reminder that I should forgive her led me to accept the way things happened at the end of my marriage, and embrace a new way of dealing with the depression." Typing a goal-oriented password every day for a month dramatically improved his mood.

The next password he chose was Quitsmoking4ever. That month Estrella did quit smoking. He told his readers that this new approach to passwords had changed his life. "Try it yourself! Write these statements with the right mindset and attitude, and you'll change your life."

Rule #2: Use Mnemonic, Goal-Setting, or Poetic Passwords

We hope you don't use weak passwords such as "123456" or "password." They're easy to remember, of course, and extremely common. In fact, researchers estimate that half of us use weak passwords, and recent data breaches confirmed this when the hackers posted stolen login credentials for the whole world to see.[2] Simple, unsafe, and easy-to-guess passwords abound. But feeble passwords pose a serious cybersecurity problem known as the password paradox: Easy-to-remember passwords are easy to break. Hard passwords are the opposite. So, how do you create a password that's easy to remember but hard to hack?

Good: Mnemonic Passwords

One approach is a mnemonic device—a pattern of letters, ideas, or associations that assist in remembering something.[3] Students use this method to remember things like the order of the planets or the colors of the spectrum. You may still recall the mnemonics you learned in school. If you can remember these catchy phrases, you can recall a strong password.

To start, you first need to pick a phrase—lyrics from a favorite song, a line from a poem or prayer, a favorite quote, or any phrase you can remember. Let's say you pick the Beatles song lyric, "Hey Jude, don't make it bad. Take a sad song and make it better."

You take the first letter from each word in the phrase and get: Hjdmibtassamib

Already that's a stronger password than "123456." But now you need to add some strength. Swap or add some characters—symbols, numbers, and uppercase letters: HJ!DmibT@$$@miB

You can make this password even stronger by bracketing the phrase with a meaningful number in your life that is not your birthday or Social Security number. For example, if you pick the date December 19, you get: 12HJ!DmibT@$$@miB19

Now you have a password that's tough for hackers to break but still easy to remember. You know the lyric by heart and the bracketed numbers mean something to you.

Better: Goal-Setting Passwords

Estrella's goal-setting password strategy (discussed in the Hack Report earlier) creates a strong but memorable password that embodies a personal goal, which works very well when you need to change your password regularly. Not only will this method help you remember your password, but every time you type it, you'll reinforce your goal, too. Of course, you'll want to beef up your password with some numbers and symbols. Some examples:

Run thirty minutes every day →Run30M!nutes3v3ryd@y
Eat more fruits and vegetables →3@t>fru1t&v3g3t@bl3s
Drink eight glasses of water → Dr!nk8Gl@$$e$ofW@+er
Lift weights twice a week → L!ftw3!ghts2x@w33k
Walk more, drive less → W@lkM0r3Dr!v3L3$$

Best: Unbreakable Passphrases and Poetry

A third and very secure way to beat the password paradox involves creating a five-word passphrase using the Diceware method. You start by rolling a die five times to create a random number. For example, say you roll 4, 1, 2, 2, and 6. Then repeat that process four more times, so you have five five-digit numbers, such as:

41226
13523
56121
23653
22143

Match each number to a word on the 7,776-word Diceware Word List found on the Internet. When you do, you get the passphrase: *lucy beau sulfa dye cuny*. Security experts believe the Diceware method creates passwords with the most strength, especially when you separate each word with a space, number, or symbol.[4]

Two University of Southern California (USC) researchers expanded on this passphrase idea by programming a computer to create short, strong, and memorable "password poems." Their program assigns random codes to 327,868 dictionary words to ultimately create a two-line verse rhyming on the last word, such as:

> Competing holy Hemingway
> complies American ballet
>> or
> The freshman center interplay
> and tracking nodded Monterrey

Experts estimate that hackers would need five million years to crack these passwords.[5]

Too Good to Use?

Expect to see more innovation. For now, email programs that limit password length, such as Microsoft Outlook's twenty-eight characters, make it impossible to use some of the stronger passphrases.[6] (Google's Gmail, on the other hand, allows up to a one-hundred-character password.)[7] Watch for limit sizes to grow in the future.

For now, you can beat the password paradox and create strong yet memorable secret phrases, especially for your financial-only email address and online banking accounts. Of course, applying these methods to any account boosts your security.

Hack-Proof Action Step #2

☐ Create stronger passwords using mnemonic, goal-setting, or poetic password approaches.

Completion date: __/__/____   Score: 5 points

For more information and guidance on creating tougher passwords, including a letter-to-symbol conversion chart, turn to page 137 of the Action Guide section.

The Two-Step Process that Stops Hackers

Help! Mugged in Madrid—
Send Money Now

HACK REPORT: One morning, Deb Fallows, author and contributing writer for the *Atlantic*, found her Gmail account running slowly. After rebooting her computer, she couldn't log in to her email. Deb's husband, James Fallows, an author and national correspondent for the *Atlantic*, opened his inbox and saw a stream of messages from family and friends asking about his wife's situation. Scrolling down, he found a poorly written email from Deb saying she'd been mugged in Madrid and needed money wired immediately. Deb Fallows had been hacked.

With help from Google, James logged in to his wife's account and discovered that six years of messages had vanished. Those included emails with colleagues, conversations between Deb and her recently deceased father, planning details about her sons' weddings, and treasured travel photos. His wife was devastated. Luckily, after some prodding of James' high-level contacts at the technology company, Google recovered the lost messages.

Ever the resourceful writer, James Fallows chronicled his wife's misadventure in an *Atlantic* essay about the growing cybersecurity perils we face.[1] He encouraged his readers to boost their security and start using stronger, unique passwords for their accounts. James finished the article by introducing his readers to a new security feature Gmail had recently added called "two-step verification," which would have blocked hackers from seizing his wife's account and deleting six years of her digital life.

Rule #3: Enable Two-Step Verification on Your Email and Financial Accounts

The range and sophistication of security threats continue to grow. Cyber criminals exploit technology to its fullest and overwhelm our meager defenses. Now we must embrace technology to make ourselves safer whenever possible.

Verify Yourself

An important new measure called two-step verification, or two-factor authentication, should be added to your login security wherever possible—especially for your email and financial accounts. This is how it works: When you start to log in to an account, you receive a short-lived, one-time passcode sent by text message, email, or phone. You must enter that code to gain access to your account. The second step of verifying yourself—confirming you are *really* you—prevents your account from being hacked because it requires two separate things: something you know (your password) and something you have in front of you (the temporary code). Even if a hacker knows your password, he won't be able to get into your account without completing the second step, entering the verification code. (Watch for companies adding voice identification—a vocal fingerprint—to the second-step process.)[2]

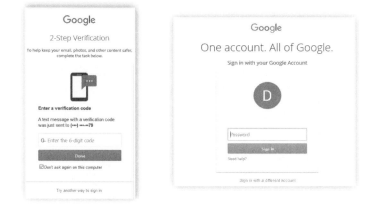

This two-step method also acts as an early-warning system. If someone has your password and attempts to log in, you will receive a code and know something is wrong. But you'll still be protected. (Nonetheless, change your password and investigate more.)

And don't worry about the potential inconvenience of the process: On most sites you can designate "safe devices." Whenever you log in to your account from a recognized computer or device, you only need to enter a code every thirty days.

Insist on Two-Step Security

In reaction to the spread of cyber threats and data breaches, expect to see more companies offering two-step verification for their services. Add this extra security to your email and online financial accounts. If this protection is not offered, register your concern and consider moving to a service that values protecting its customers.

Hack-Proof Action Step #3

☐ Enable two-step verification on all your key accounts that allow it—financial accounts and personal email.

Completion date: __/__/____   Score: 5 points

For additional direction on how to set up two-step security for your banking, credit cards, and email, consult page 138 of the Action Guide.

4

Too Many Passwords and the Unbreakable Solution

Starbucks Customers Learn the Bitter Taste of Recycled Passwords

HACK REPORT: For ease, many of us create the same username and password for different websites, a dangerous practice. In the beginning, you think: *What does it matter if someone hacks my Yelp or ESPN account? No real danger there.* But then the recycling becomes a habit. Each new website gets the same old credentials. Finally, your convenient approach to creating new accounts extends to a site that involves a small financial transaction, and then trouble ensues. If you repeat your favorite login at dozens of websites, eventually the combination will land on the black market, where hackers can turn your password into fast cash. That's what happened to some Starbucks customers who used the coffee company's mobile payment app.

Applying login combinations stolen in a data breach, hackers used "brute force attacks" against the Starbucks app, testing hundreds of names per second.[1] Because Starbucks didn't limit the number of failed sign-in attempts per account, the hackers' program kept grinding away, testing, testing, testing until it succeeded. Once the criminals controlled the customer's payment app, they just needed to transfer the account money to an untraceable gift card. If a hacked payment app automatically refilled the low account with more money, the hackers would quickly repeat their theft until the customer discovered the scam.

In a statement, Starbucks said: "To protect their security, customers are encouraged to use different user names and passwords for different sites, especially those that keep financial information."

Rule #4: Use a Password Manager for Unbreakable Protection

Before the Internet, few of us had passwords. As a kid, you probably had a bike lock and a school locker with a combination that you needed to remember. Security became more challenging with our first bank card and automated teller machine (ATM)—we needed to remember a passcode.

Then along came CompuServe and AOL, and many of us started our first online account that required a password. Before long, the World Wide Web exploded, and we've been adding accounts and passwords to our lives ever since.

In the beginning, some of us tracked these secret words by scribbling on sticky notes attached to our computers. Others stored their passwords in little black books—some still do. But tracking our passwords became an annoyance, even a burden. And smartphones and tablets just increased the number of places we could access the Internet. You can see why people came to rely on easy-to-remember passwords.

But reusing your passwords is not worth the risk. Good cyber-security trumps all, especially in the age of spammers, hackers, and identity thieves. Security experts say your online safety is only as good as the strength of your usernames and passwords. And because it's impossible to remember strong, unique passwords for the ever-growing number of sites you use, we recommend you add a password manager to your digital life—something many security experts use, too.

Only One Password to Remember

Password managers allow you to store your passwords in an encrypted file on your computer or in "the cloud," the Internet-connected computers that store digital files for on-demand access from any device. A password manager protects all your passwords with one master password. That way, you only need to remember that one secret word. But it had better be a good one! We showed you how in chapter 2.

Running a password manager allows you to stop worrying about reusing weak username and password combinations and can give you unbreakable passwords you don't need to remember. After you've set up your password manager, you log in with your master password. When you visit a website, the manager will autofill the username and password fields. If you visit a site that is not stored in your password manager, you'll get help creating a new, strong password with a couple of clicks.

Adding a password manager service will cost you from $10 to $30 annually, and you can sync your manager to your computers, smartphones, and tablets. That's a small price to pay for super-strong encrypted passwords you don't need to remember. Look at it as an inexpensive insurance policy.[2]

Are Password Managers Safe?

Some people worry that their manager could get hacked, exposing their passwords, but that fear is unfounded. First, password managers encrypt their subscribers' password files, so even the company that developed the program can't access your secret codes, including your master password. Second, hackers would have to break each heavily encrypted password separately—a daunting prospect with low return on their investment of time. Finally, in the unlikely event that hackers should break in to a password manager and decrypt your password file, you'd still be safe, because two-step verification on your financial accounts would alert you to the problem and block the thieves from getting in.

Now you see why adding a password manager to your digital life makes sense, right? It's an important step to boost your security. Plus, a password manager reduces your need to create, track, and remember strong passwords.

Hack-Proof Action Step #4

☐ Download a password manager and put it on all your computers and devices. Pick a strong master password using the mnemonic or poetic approach.

Completion date: __/__/____   Score: 5 points

To get started picking a password manager, turn to page 141 of the Action Guide to read our summaries of the popular programs.

The Danger of Free Public Wi-Fi: It's a Honeypot for Hackers

The British Politicians
Who Loved Free Wi-Fi Too Much

HACK REPORT: Everyone enjoys free things, especially Internet access. But free does not mean safe, as three British politicians demonstrated. The officials, all enthusiastic promoters of no-cost public Wi-Fi, volunteered to participate in an experiment designed to show the risk and danger of complimentary wireless. It did not go well for the politicians.

All three suffered a different type of cyber attack over free connectivity, according to *Hacker News*, which reported the results of the experiment conducted jointly by several security firms—good guys pretending to be hackers.[1] The first, David Davis, lost control of his email account when researchers secretly recorded his username and password. Later, they entered his PayPal account—an easy hack, because Davis used the same login credentials for Gmail and PayPal. "Well, it is pretty horrifying, to be honest," Davis told the researchers conducting the experiment. "What you have extracted was a very tough password, tougher than most people use. It is certainly not 'Password.'"

The next politician, Mary Honeyball, fell for a phishing attack while sipping coffee and using wireless in a café. The hackers created a fake Facebook login message and sent it to Honeyball's laptop. She took the bait, and then the hackers took over her Facebook account. (In her role as a British member of the European Parliament, Honeyball also served on the committee promoting the European Union's "We love Wi-Fi" campaign. Ouch!)

Lord Paul Strasburger, the third politician, encountered trouble by making a simple Voice Over Internet Protocol (VoIP) phone call from his hotel room using a free connection. The researchers listened and recorded his conversation.

The politicians demonstrated the chief reason for the experiment: People don't know how to safely use open, no-charge wireless. These officials said that they often used public Internet connections but never received any formal training on its dangers. Fortunately, they learned the hazards of open, free Wi-Fi before suffering a real malicious attack from hackers.

Rule #5: Use Free Public Wi-Fi with Extreme Caution

For many of us, connecting to the Internet seems as vital as food, water, and air. Yet online access wasn't always so easy or available. In earlier days, you could only get online through a work computer physically connected to the Internet. If you wanted access at home, you needed a computer modem to dial out and connect to the Internet—a slow and tedious experience.

But our love of and fascination with the Internet grew with the introduction of wireless connections. A well-placed router beamed a signal to your laptop and you just clicked an icon and connected—so much easier than dial-up modems.

Soon people wanted access beyond the home or office: gyms, pools, cafés, hotels, libraries—everywhere. Wireless hotspots sprouted like mushrooms and provided instant connectivity for our laptops and smartphones—no password or network key required. Fantastic!

Naturally, the hackers celebrated, too, because free Wi-Fi had little or no security, and more people connecting in more places created new potential victims. Hackers could use a simple eavesdropping tool to spy on people using free, unsecured wireless hotspots. A hacker could sit as far as a hundred feet away and watch and record all that you do, stealing your personal information whenever you log in to your email or bank account and infecting your computer with malicious software.[2] So we must temper our enthusiasm for free Internet. Cyber thieves see it as a honeypot attracting new victims, but you must view it as a hornet's nest of potential trouble.

Three Choices for Free Wi-Fi

If you absolutely must use a free hotspot, proceed cautiously and follow these guidelines:

1. If you connect to free, unsecured Wi-Fi with your device, you face several risks, including being monitored by a hacker or catching a spyware virus that might record any username and password you enter. So you don't want to log in to your email, make any online purchases, or enter any financial website while using the unsafe connection. (Other cybersecurity rules you'll learn later may give you additional protection here, but it remains unwise to conduct serious business on free wireless.)

2. If you must take the risk, you need a software program called a Virtual Private Network (VPN) to protect your online activity and identity. By adding a VPN to your laptop, smartphone, or tablet, you'll have a secure connection over free wireless Internet to access sensitive and private accounts—email or your bank account—even while on free wireless. When you only have public Internet, you simply launch the program when you connect to the signal. The VPN will create your own secure, private network over the Internet and encrypt any data you share. Hackers can't eavesdrop while you log in to your email or bank account.

If you're in a sensitive personal or business situation, your security will improve dramatically by launching the private network when you connect over free Wi-Fi.[3]

3. Your other option involves turning your smartphone into a temporary hotspot. In this case, you don't use the free connectivity and you get temporary, secure Internet access. Anytime you turn your smartphone service (AT&T, Verizon, Sprint, etc.) into a Wi-Fi access point, you have a safe, encrypted connection. If you're in a pinch and need to get online, this option will work.

Free wireless is a great convenience, but the hackers love it, too. Stay safe and take precautions when connecting.

Hack-Proof Action Step #5

☐ Install a VPN program on your laptop and mobile devices for safe use of free Wi-Fi.

Completion date: __/__/____   Score: 5 points

You have many options for adding a virtual network. Turn to page 143 of our Action Guide, where you'll see a list of choices and also find advice about setting up your smartphone as a secure wireless hotspot.

"Good Fences Make Good Neighbors" Applies to Your Home Wi-Fi Network

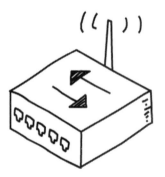

The Mystery of the Wi-Fi Hacker
and the Illegal Downloads

HACK REPORT: How would you feel if you opened your mail one morning and discovered a cease-and-desist letter claiming you'd illegally downloaded copyrighted material? That's what happened to a neighbor of Roger Grimes, a security writer at *InfoWorld*.[1]

The legal notice shocked the woman, and she immediately contacted Grimes, knowing he understood the Internet. Grimes assumed full detective mode. First, he scanned her computer for viruses. Nothing. Then he checked her home Wi-Fi router. She had followed security guidelines, changed the default password, and kept her login credentials secret. But when Grimes audited her router, he uncovered a clue. Someone was regularly using her connection—the illegal downloader.

Grimes took immediate action. He reset the router and changed the username and password to something even stronger. That seemed to work for a few weeks, until the Hollywood company sent another cease-and-desist letter with a more threatening demand—get a lawyer.

Grimes returned to his neighbor's home and finally concluded she'd been victimized by a rare case of "WPS hacking." WPS stands for Wi-Fi Protected Setup, which is a function on all routers. Engineers created WPS for good reason: It allows devices to easily connect to a wireless network. But that convenience puts people at risk.

A hacker can break a WPS passcode with the right attack tool, a password-guessing program. Grimes realized that is exactly what happened to his neighbor. So he put a stop to the illegal downloading by logging in to the woman's router and clicking "Disable WPS." Simple solution.

Later, as he explained in his *InfoWorld* column, he helped other neighbors close similar wireless security holes. "I updated everyone's router firmware code (none of them were even remotely up to date), changed any default passwords I found, and either disabled their WPS-feature or made sure that the guessing lockout feature was enabled," he wrote. The hackers would need to find another neighborhood to victimize.

Rule #6: Secure Your Home Wi-Fi Network to Keep Out Hackers

In the age of the Internet, modern home security now requires that you prevent virtual intruders, too. That starts by securing your home wireless network to protect your data and devices—a measure people often overlook.

To keep the hackers out, you need to complete a security check on your router and carry out four security actions:

1. Change your router's default username and password.

2. Encrypt your router.

3. Disable the Wi-Fi Protected Setup (WPS) feature.

4. Update the router's software.

But don't be alarmed. These actions take just a couple of minutes. If you need help, consult our Action Guide in the back.

Boosting Your Wireless Security

First, you want to give your router its own custom password and username—the name you see when you select a wireless signal to get on the Internet. Make sure you don't have the router's original name and password given at the factory. Hackers know the manufacturers' default settings and will easily break in if you don't change them.

Second, you need to select the strongest encryption for your router—either WPA or WPA2. WPA stands for Wi-Fi Protected Access and WPA2 is the second generation of the feature. Both options offer very strong protection and will keep hackers from penetrating your network. If your router only offers the older, standard protection called WEP—Wired Equivalent Privacy—then you need to purchase a new one. Security experts no longer believe WEP offers strong protection.[2]

Don't Let Them Guess

Third, you want to prevent hackers from trying to guess your wireless password. You can do this by disabling the WPS (Wi-Fi Protected Setup) feature on your Wi-Fi router or putting a limit on the number of guesses someone can take before gaining access. Either approach will give you stronger security.[3]

Your fourth action involves updating your Wi-Fi router's operating software, which is called "firmware." This is a simple action similar to updating software on your computer or devices. If you run out-of-date software, hackers could exploit security holes to enter your network.[4] (Later, in chapter 14, we'll spend more time explaining the connection between software updates and enhanced cybersecurity.)

Now you've taken another step toward boosting your cybersecurity. You know how to secure your wireless network, and you'll never have virtual trespassers illegally downloading files on your Wi-Fi network.

Hack-Proof Action Step #6

☐ Change your router's default username and password—don't keep the factory settings.

☐ Select the WPA or WPA2 encryption setting.

☐ Disable the WPS setting on your router.

☐ Update your router's software.

Completion date: __/__/____   Score: 5 points

For more details and assistance on making security changes to your wireless router, turn to page 144 of the Action Guide.

7

Protect Your Phone and Tablet: Track Them like a Bounty Hunter

The "Lost" Smartphone
and the Good Samaritan

HACK REPORT: If you found a smartphone, would you pick it up? If you picked it up, would you turn it on? What next?

Security firm Symantec wanted to learn what you might do, and for good reason: Millions of phones are lost or stolen each year, and many have no security. So it created an experiment called the Smartphone Honey Stick Project.[1] The company wanted to learn exactly what people would do if we suddenly came upon a smartphone, clearly lost and unclaimed. What types of information would we try to access?

Here's what Symantec did. The company "lost" fifty Android smartphones in five North American cities. They intentionally put them in places where they'd be found: elevators, shopping malls, food courts, and other spots with lots of people.

The phones had no security passcodes to stop people from taking a "deep dive" into the owner's digital life. Symantec configured each device with a simulated owner's contact information and tracking software to follow the device's movement.

What happened next may shock you. The people who picked up the lost smartphones pried deeply into the phone owners' lives:

- 89 percent opened personal apps and data, including online banking

- 83 percent tapped on business information

- 72 percent viewed photos

- 60 percent snooped into social networks and email accounts

- 57 percent tried to open a Saved Passwords file

Perhaps the saddest result involved 50 percent of the Good Samaritans who actually made an honest effort to contact the phone's owner. Half of them also spent time viewing people's personal information.

While we tend to think of cybersecurity in terms of anonymous hackers using the Internet to perpetrate their frauds and scams, the Symantec study showed something more: We need to guard our data-filled devices from the average human threat, too.

As the experiment revealed, if a stranger finds your lost, unprotected smartphone, your sensitive personal- and business-related information likely will be inspected. Plus, there's no guarantee the finder will return it, even with your contact information in plain view. Your devices need security.

Rule #7: Protect Your Smartphone and Tablet with Passcodes

Have you noticed how people covet their smartphones? They've become fashion statements and status symbols. But they're no ordinary bauble. We use them for more than phone calls: we text, shop, email, play games, navigate, read articles and books, and make video and audio recordings. (The Apple and Google app stores alone each supply more than 1.5 million smartphone and tablet programs!)[2]

But thieves want your smartphones and tablets, too, and steal nearly two million devices each year. Yet one-third of smartphone owners still don't protect their phones, even though the devices amount to an open diary of their lives.[3] That must change.

Secure Your Phone and Tablet

Here's what you need to do: Put a passcode lock on your phone and tablet—the most basic security precaution and a critical barrier between a thief and your personal information. Adding a passcode only takes a few seconds, and it protects your sensitive data. Just go to Settings on your devices. For Apple users, complete the process in General, then Restrictions. Samsung and other Android users can do the same under Quick Settings, then Screen Lock, or Location & Security, then Set Up Lock Screen. Simple.

Two Additional Precautions

You're not done yet. When smartphones first hit the market, theft soared to over three million per year. Manufacturers took note and realized their devices needed better security, so they added tracking apps called Find My iPhone and Locate My Phone. Be sure you activate that app so you can locate a lost or stolen device.

While researching this book, we discovered that some people objected to using a passcode for safety reasons. They worried that someone couldn't identify their emergency contacts in case of accident or illness. But that's no longer true. You can still have security on your smartphone and allow access to your emergency contacts, too. Just complete your Medical ID screen in the iPhone Health app. For Android users, complete the In Case of Emergency fields under Security in your Settings app.[4]

You never know when you may part ways with your device, so add the simple protections that will keep snooping eyes out of your personal data and even help you recover a lost or stolen phone or tablet. You'll feel more secure, even in a bad situation.

Hack-Proof Action Step #7

☐ Create passcodes for your smartphones and tablets.

☐ Activate the Find My iPhone or Locate My Phone app in case your device becomes lost or stolen.

☐ Add your emergency contact information to your devices.

Completion date: __/__/____   Score: 5 points

For more details about using passcodes and other safety and security features for your devices, turn to page 150 in the Action Guide section.

8

How to Stop Identity Theft on Facebook and Other Social Media

Woman Learns the Price of Overlooking Privacy Settings—Identity Theft

HACK REPORT: Victoria Sennitt always guarded her identity closely. She routinely shredded any bills or other documents that included her name, address, date of birth, and other facts about her life. But when social media exploded and her friends started joining Facebook, Sennitt jumped right in, according to the *Daily Mail.*[1] She completed her profile with as much information as possible, thinking it felt safe and that only friends could see her information and posts.

One day, Sennitt received a letter in the morning mail. It contained a contract for cell phone service—except Sennitt had never signed such a contract. With a sinking feeling, she quickly realized someone had successfully impersonated her.

How could this have happened? Sennitt believed she'd always been cautious about sharing her personal data. Except on Facebook, where she'd posted for all to see: her name, address, birth date, and phone number—enough details for a thief to "scrape" her personal information and obtain a cell phone in her name.

Luckily, Sennitt proved she'd been scammed and the phone company canceled the contract. But because she didn't understand how privacy settings worked on Facebook, she'd suffered an identity theft—and now the hackers possessed her personal data.

Rule #8: Tighten Your Social Media Privacy Settings

Sharing is a core value of social media and a key reason for the wild growth and success of companies such as Facebook, Twitter, YouTube, and LinkedIn. For some of us, it's fun to post comments, articles, photos, and videos for our friends and social media followers. Many people participate passively, watching and reading others' posts but rarely sharing their own. Never have humans had such open and easy access to tell their personal stories or share their ideas, experiences, and feelings.

But like much about the Internet, all this sharing can draw unwanted and dangerous attention. You don't want the "bad guys" watching you. And any social media platform you use potentially connects you to mind-boggling numbers of people. Over a billion people worldwide have a Facebook account[2], 307 million people actively use Twitter[3], and the number of Instagram users exceeds 500 million.[4] That's why you must exercise complete control over your digital life, and you do that on social media by keeping a sharp eye on your privacy settings. Nearly all social media sites let you control who sees your information. When you review your privacy controls regularly, you ensure that you have the strongest security in place.

Who Can See Your Profile?

Social media networks continue to grow and allow you to connect with family, friends, colleagues, and classmates, but sharing without thinking about who sees your information just invites trouble.

We often ask people we meet if they've checked their social media privacy settings lately—many have no idea. That usually means the public can view their open profiles—posts, photos, likes, friends, and other activities. You may be OK with that openness, but you should be concerned.

Scammers can "scrape" or copy your profile, learn more about you, and use that information to perpetrate any variety of scams, frauds, and hacks. For example, say you post a photo of your dog in your backyard and write a caption such as "Look at Buddy soaking up the sun." A scammer who reads that post now has a good chance of answering the password reset question on your email account if you selected: "What's your pet's name?" An open profile gives hackers the important details they need to hack your life—whether it's seizing your email account, assuming your identity in credit-card fraud, or cracking your bank account.[5] Strong privacy settings block hackers from seeing your profiles.

Know Your Privacy Settings and Your Friends

You can still enjoy social media and maintain good security, you just need to strike the right balance by knowing how privacy settings work at different sites. A simple Google search on a website's name and "privacy settings" will get you started. All social media sites will give you some measure of control over who sees your profile and activities. Your biggest decision will be selecting a security level that allows you to share with friends while keeping your privacy. Thankfully, it won't involve much effort.

In addition to beefing up your privacy settings, you'll also need to review your "friends" to make sure you still want them to see your social media activities. For example, should the friend of a friend know when you are on vacation because they can see your photos? It's important to remember that your posts have a larger audience than you realize. Also, social media companies frequently change their privacy policies and default settings. Pay attention to privacy updates you receive from Facebook and other sites: They're not just "fine print" and often contain important changes that need your attention if you want to keep strong privacy on social media.

We think most people should follow this rule: Do not leave your profile open for everyone to see. A study by antivirus firm Norton found that four in every ten social media users have suffered fraud.[6] Open profiles essentially hand over your personal information to scammers and hackers without much effort. Don't make their job easy. Think twice about what you share and with whom—a key rule to hack-proofing your life.

Hack-Proof Action Step #8

☐ Review and strengthen your social media privacy settings.
☐ Reexamine your "friends" to ensure you're still comfortable sharing with them.

Completion date: __/__/____   Score: 5 points

For complete details on finding the privacy settings at the most popular social media sites, turn to page 153 of the Action Guide section.

PART II

Omniscience

Your Brain against the Hackers

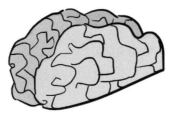

When we talk about online security, we mean guarding your personal information that acts as your surrogate on the Internet—the "digital you." For instance, *you* can't physically shop at eBay, only an Internet-connected device that *represents you* can conduct online commerce, an amazing innovation. Hackers also marvel at Internet innovation because it makes impersonating you easy. Once they've stolen your personal data, in no time they can assume your identity and start draining your bank account, run up your credit card, and spoil your credit history. They can wreak havoc in your life.

So, why don't we worry more about cybersecurity—a persistent risk to our safety that could cause hours, days, even weeks of anxiety and headache? We know from experience that a simple call to our friendly personal banker won't erase the impact of a hack or identity theft, right? And every day the headlines warn us of the dangers we face, yet many people seem paralyzed to act—even as friends, family, and colleagues get ensnared by cyber attacks. This kind of human behavior hurts. But why?

Well, neuroscientists and psychologists tell us our brains follow built-in patterns—weaknesses, actually—that make cybersecurity a challenge. Our gray matter acts against keeping us safe, even though, as you'll soon see, we can learn to turn that weakness into strength. So, before we learn the next group of New Cybersecurity Rules, we need to know how our brain and security interact—a critical insight necessary for assuming an all-knowing position over our online financial lives.

The Psychology of Security

People's idea of security has at least two sides, according to security expert and author Bruce Schneier: "Security is both a feeling and a reality. And they're not the same." On one side, we equate security with feeling safe; on the other, we view security as specific actions we take to reduce or eliminate threats. Each side reflects very different aspects of security.

For instance, you may know people who feel safe and protected at home. Their great sense of comfort and security extends to leaving their doors and windows unlocked. They know their neighborhood and believe it totally safe. But strong *feelings* of security can't erase reality, right? At any time, thieves could enter their unprotected homes.

So we have a disconnect between feelings and reality. Ideally, you can *feel* secure and *be* secure—a state we want to achieve and sustain. But Schneier says a problem arises when feelings of security don't match reality. Why? In essence, we are bad judges of risk.

Psychology reveals three struggles we confront to stay safe. First, we suffer from what social scientists call "optimism bias." People don't think they face risk. We irrationally believe that only other people face serious risks, but not us. Second, we lack motivation and urgency. Many of us think: *It wasn't a problem in the past. Why would it be now?* And third, no one rewards our security. We may proudly display status symbols of power, wealth, or success, but we can't easily show off our excellent and invisible cybersecurity.

The Risk and Reward Duel

When contemplating security, our brain hosts a quiet fight between risk and reward to determine acceptable trade-offs: We get something and we give up something. But if we badly estimate the *severity* of a risk, we get the *trade-off* wrong. As Schneier says, "Assessing and reacting to risk is one of the most important things a living creature has to deal with."

A framework people use to measure risk typically involves answering questions in their head about:

- How dangerous are the consequences of a risk?

- What's the likelihood of a negative outcome?

- How much time, money, pain, and discomfort will it take to fix what might go wrong?

- How good are the things designed to reduce my risk?

After that quick assessment, experts say we end the process with one final question: What can I safely get away with?[1]

Thinking about security is complicated. Over time, we've all made security trade-offs. Usually we start with little or no security, but later we consent to giving up convenience or comfort in return for greater protection. For instance, with tobacco, we accepted filtered cigarettes, then health warnings, and smoking bans. At home, we implemented house locks, then alarm systems, and now even remote webcams. For the car, we agreed to seat belts, then airbags, and soon, maybe even driverless cars—who knows? We made these rational decisions both at the societal and individual level.

But as humans, we're not 100-percent-rational beings. We also make irrational security trade-offs, such as fear of flying versus driving.

Plane crashes kill hundreds every year while deaths from car accidents exceed forty thousand in the U.S. alone.[2] However, everyone knows someone who won't fly. Similar irrational trade-offs abound. Why?

People get caught up and respond to exaggerated, rare risks while downplaying common risks, scientists say. For instance, many of us tend to perceive terrorists as more dangerous than an unknown, local burglar. "We worry about the wrong things, paying too much attention to minor risks and not enough attention to major ones," says Schneier.

Two Systems for Reacting to Risk

Part of the problem involves our brain using two systems to assess risk: a primitive, intuitive system found in the amygdala and an advanced, analytic system found in the neocortex. The two brain systems operate in parallel and not as equal partners. The older amygdala strikes quickly, often long before the more rational neocortex engages.[3] This mismatch demonstrates an evolutionary failing: Sometimes we can't shake our caveman instincts, and that causes un-caveman-like trouble.

Our social and technological advancement has outpaced our progress as a species. Think about it. Squirrels can outmaneuver dogs and cats but not speeding cars. Pigeons can ditch hawks but not the spray of shotgun pellets. Whales can swim the seven seas but not evade the hunter's cannon-powered harpoons. As humans, we, too, face new situations that didn't exist ten thousand years ago—or even ten years ago! Our brains have not kept up with the demands of the Internet.

Financial Omniscience

How can we use our head to hack-proof our lives? Our answer, as you'll read in this section's chapters, involves using technology to achieve a position of omniscience, or all-knowingness, over your financial affairs. By following the New Cybersecurity Rules, you'll keep your brain primed and alert to what's happening in your digital world.

Only from a current, fully informed position can you exercise greater security over your financial life. You'll keep your eye on your finances at all times and you'll know when money leaves your accounts. You will completely control your credit, not the credit-card companies or identity thieves. If you have minor children, you'll guard their credit, too. You will even understand how to spot an ATM fraud.

Remember, only the *real* you can protect your digital identity. But you must take action. We're going to show you how. So, let's take the next steps in boosting your Cybersecurity Score.

9

Track Your
Money in Motion,
Just Like the Banks Do

Woman's Black-Friday Target Deals Deliver a Black-Christmas Surprise

HACK REPORT: How would you feel to discover hackers had plundered your bank account for nearly $1,000 on Christmas Eve? "It was a very empty feeling," Leslie Frederickson told *ABC7 News*, shortly after the theft.[1] The San Francisco television station had been covering the aftermath of the 2013 data breach of the discount retailer Target, and she was the ideal subject to demonstrate the hack's impact and show viewers one way to limit their harm in such a scam.

Frederickson's trouble started about one month earlier on Black Friday. Like many people, she had shopped at her local Target the day after Thanksgiving and nabbed a few money-saving Christmas deals. All seemed well until a week before Christmas when the Target data breach news broke.

The cyber thieves had put credit- and debit-card numbers and other personal information on the black market, opening more than 110 million Target customers to possible fraud. The successful heist turned into an early Christmas for the data scammers. For Frederickson, Christmas cheer ended when her bank advised that she was overdrawn by $100. That seemed odd. Frederickson knew she had enough money to cover her upcoming rent and pay for some last-minute Christmas expenses. *The insufficient funds notice must be a problem with the bank*, Frederickson thought. However, it wasn't.

She quickly learned that a fraudster in Utah had used her debit-card number four times for $850 in charges, with the final expenditure pushing the account into overdraft, triggering the bank alert.

Now Frederickson had to borrow money to pay for Christmas dinner and the January rent. When she tried to speed up the process, the bank denied her request. Desperate, Frederickson turned to the *ABC7 News* consumer advocate who had put her story on the air. The bank quickly changed course and she got her money back, but not until after a three-week wait and a ruined Christmas.

Rule #9: Set Text or Email Alerts for Bank Accounts and Credit Cards

In a data breach, cyber thieves exploit security holes in a company's network to steal customer data to sell on the black market or use for identity theft and credit-card fraud. When we hear the news of another corporate data breach, we often can't comprehend the magnitude and potential danger. One month hackers steal two million names, the next it's twelve million, and so on. The numbers keep changing like a weird Powerball lottery in which the hackers always win and the rest of us lose. Over the last decade, corporate data breaches finally exceeded a jaw-dropping one billion stolen customer records: addresses, birth dates, credit card, debit card, Social Security numbers, and other unique personal facts.[2] Hackers likely swept up some of your personal data in that ongoing crime wave.

No one can avoid the stark reality that in recent years cyber criminals have collectively breached just about everyone's privacy. That means that in order to hack-proof your life, you must operate from the belief that you are vulnerable to impersonation and identity theft right now. To take new actions to regain your security and privacy, you must assume a role of omniscience—all-knowingness—over your financial affairs.

One key approach to enhancing your cybersecurity involves using technology to your advantage by putting text or email alerts on your financial accounts. If the banks and credit-card companies can know your financial situation up to the minute, why shouldn't you?

Alerts empower you to know the activity happening on your bank account and credit cards at all times. By receiving an alert text or email when the bank allows money to leave your account or when your credit card is charged, you'll be able to spot fraud as it happens.

The Liability Question

Keeping your eye out for suspicious charges can save you some money, too. If you don't get alert notifications and miss a fraudulent charge, you could be on the hook for that loss. For your debit card, if you report fraud within forty-eight hours, you're only liable for up to $50. However, after two days your liability jumps to $500. Report the fraud more than two months after receiving your bank statement, and you could be liable for all charges. For credit cards, your liability maxes out at $50—no matter when you report the fraud.[3]

Make Technology Work for You

You can set up alert notification systems when you log in or create your online accounts at your bank or credit-card companies. In most cases, you decide what dollar amount triggers an alert. For example, you can choose to get notified only when a charge exceeds $100. We recommend setting up alerts for all transactions, no matter the amount. Thieves commonly test accounts by making small charges before reaching for larger amounts. The sooner you catch them, the better. Just contact customer service for help.

If your financial institutions don't offer notifications, move your business elsewhere. You can't achieve omniscience over your financial affairs if the only alert you ever receive is an overdraft notification.

Hack-Proof Action Step #9

☐ Create text or email alerts for your bank accounts and credit cards.

Completion date: __/__/____   Score: 5 points

Banks and credit-card companies have different approaches to setting alerts on accounts. For more details, turn to page 156 in the Action Guide section.

10

A Simple Way to Stop Identity Theft and Protect Your Good Name

The Army Major's
Welcome-Home Shock—
a Stolen Identity

HACK REPORT: Retired army major John Smith knew a military career brought its own special risks, but he didn't know those would include losing his identity. After Smith returned from a three-year post in Germany, he wanted to buy a home. Low interest rates meant this was a favorable time to apply for a mortgage. Plus, Smith knew he had a good credit rating.

But he didn't. "They told me I had a horrible credit record," Smith told the Army News Service, which spread the soldier's story using a pseudonym to protect his identity. "I couldn't believe it. I never missed a payment on anything."

When he requested a copy of his credit report, Smith saw the problem: He'd been victimized by an identity thief. His file detailed a string of delinquent charges stretching across the map from Tennessee, Kentucky, Colorado, New Mexico, Arizona, and California.

While Smith had been living and working overseas as a physician's assistant, his impersonator back home forged Smith's name, Social Security number, and past addresses to assume a new identity in order to rack up cell phone, credit card, and department store charges that never got paid.

When the major discovered the fraud, he launched what would become a ten-year struggle to clear his name, rebuild his credit, and regain his identity. Smith never paid a cent on the ill-gotten debt, but he filled a double-drawer file cabinet with reports and records proving to unpaid creditors that an identity thief had incurred the debts. Smith took his story to the Army News Service because he wanted others to benefit from his experience: "Protect your identity. Limit how much information you give out. And check your credit report once or twice a year. I made the mistake of not checking my credit annually, especially while I was overseas. If I had, I may have been able to catch the problem sooner and nip it in the bud."[1]

Rule #10: Put a Security Freeze on Your Credit Files

Not everyone fully understands the nuances of managing his or her credit. That said, you must gain more knowledge, and exercise more control and awareness about protecting your credit files, if you want to hack-proof your life.

We've all heard the old phrase "Money makes the world go round," but replacing "money" with "credit" better describes reality. Credit greases the wheels of the global economic system. The banking world invites our participation from early adulthood, offering us easy lines of credit to charge whatever we desire. Receiving credit is a heady rite of passage in our consumer-driven world, one filled with fine print, terms and conditions, and other hidden rules and charges we rarely consider.

One reason the credit system succeeds so well is something economists call "low friction." The big three credit-reporting agencies place our files, by default, in the most open and unsecured setting, which makes it easy for people to obtain new lines of credit in their name. You complete an application, and if you meet a lender's criteria, you're approved!

The lightly guarded credit process works for everyone, lenders and consumers—plus, hackers and identity thieves, too. The system's openness makes it ripe for fraud and abuse. The numbers bear this out. Security researchers estimate that cyber criminals produce a new identity theft victim every two seconds—more than thirteen million per year.[2]

Identity theft can occur in many ways, though usually the primary crime arises from a data breach—the wholesale theft of thousands, hundreds of thousands, or millions of people's personal identifying records. The data pilfering sets up a second phase of wrongdoing: widespread individual identity theft. Scammers steal people's identities relatively easily, if their credit files are open—a fairly common situation. The fraudster simply uses some portion of your stolen personal information—date of birth and Social Security number, for instance—as the basis for gaining new credit in your name without your knowledge. Your unprotected credit file invites trouble.

You Need a Security Freeze at the Three Credit Bureaus

A simple action will secure your credit record. You just need to put your files at all three credit-reporting agencies on something called a Security Freeze, more commonly known as a Credit Freeze, the most secure of three anti-fraud controls offered.[3]

The two other more publicized settings, Credit Monitoring and Fraud Alert, don't provide the strong, lasting protection you need to hack-proof your life. Credit Monitoring won't stop a thief from opening new credit in your name because the control only alerts you to potential fraud *after* the fact.[4] You'll still have to put in the hours to report the incident and get your record corrected. Who wants that?

The other setting, Fraud Alert, provides more protection than Credit Monitoring, but only for a short while. If suspected fraudulent activity already exists on your credit files, a Fraud Alert will notify you about any new attempt to place more credit in your name. But the alert expires in ninety days and will need to be renewed to continue—not very helpful or convenient.

A Security Freeze is your only sensible and safe option. Freezing your credit locks your credit files with a PIN that only you know, and prevents the reporting bureaus from releasing your files to any lender seeking to view your credit history. To receive new credit, you just unfreeze the files with your PIN. (After lifting the freeze and securing new credit, return your files to Security Freeze for continued protection.)

A Security Freeze gives you complete control of your credit. You, and only you, approve adding new credit in your name. But you must freeze your file at all three credit-reporting agencies: Equifax, Experian, and TransUnion. Adding this security measure costs very little—from free to $10 at each bureau. (Similar charges apply to lifting a freeze.)

Keep Watching

Once you protect your credit files you can rest easier—but still keep a watchful eye. One-fourth of American adults have never checked their credit report, meaning many people don't know whether identity thieves have already impersonated them.[5] Remember, the law entitles you to one free credit report from all three credit bureaus each year, so make sure you check your reports annually for discrepancies.

Now that you understand the meaning of a Security Freeze, hopefully you can see why taking control of your credit files is critical in the defense against identity theft and a key step in becoming omniscient about your financial life.

Hack-Proof Action Step #10

☐ Place a Security Freeze on your credit files at all three reporting agencies: Equifax, Experian, and TransUnion.

Completion date: __/__/____   Score: 5 points

For more guidance on putting your Security Freeze in place and monitoring your credit files, turn to page 157 in the Action Guide section.

One Thing Parents Must Do to Protect Their Children from Identity Theft

Boy's Childhood Identity Theft
Hounds Him into Adulthood

HACK REPORT: Jeri Marks' excitement for her young son's modeling career quickly turned into a modern nightmare and not the type of model she expected. When Marks filed the 11-year-old boy's first tax return, the Internal Revenue Service (IRS) uncovered a problem. A return under his Social Security number already existed. Ever since, the scourge of a persistent identity theft has haunted the woman and her son, Gabriel Jimenez.

Even though she notified the police, the Social Security Administration, and the IRS, the fraud continued. Several years later, Marks learned from her son's IRS file that an illegal immigrant had stolen the boy's Social Security number and was still using it. She even tracked down the impersonator, who offered to hand over his annual tax refund if he could continue to use the number.

Into adulthood, Jimenez's troubles continued. He told the *New York Times* of his difficulty setting up bank accounts and getting approved for car insurance.[1] Utility companies denied him credit when Jimenez tried to set up phone, gas, and electricity for his first apartment because the thief had already created accounts under his Social Security number. The problem meant he could only rent utilities-included apartments. Time after time Jimenez had to prove his own identity, long after locating the thief and getting him to stop using the stolen Social Security number.

Rule #11: Confirm Your Children Have No Unauthorized Credit Reports

Good cybersecurity requires you monitor more than just your own credit files. Your children's unblemished names represent serious, lucrative credit-fraud opportunities for identity thieves, and need protection only you can deliver. So our call to hack-proof your life and become all-knowing about your financial affairs also extends to your minor children. Identity thieves target them, too.

Experts say that child identity thefts continue to rise, though researchers find it difficult to estimate the size of the problem for the very reason the criminals love stealing kids' identities: Parents rarely check their children's names at the credit-reporting companies—the only way to spot and confirm a fraud—which means the impersonations go unnoticed and unreported for years.[2]

The lapse by parents makes sense: We don't naturally think to check the credit rating of our minor children, since we know they have no credit. But if a thief possesses a child's Social Security number, he can use an unspoiled identity as the basis for bank accounts, credit cards, insurance, loans, and employment.

Worse, the impersonator can ruin a child's credit history by never paying bills and taxes, and even creating a criminal record. Only later, when an older child applies for a college loan, apartment lease, or credit card, would a low credit score and identity theft come to light, and clearing one's name can be difficult and time consuming.

The Catch-22 of Spotting Child Identity Theft

To ensure your child does not start adulthood a victim of identity theft, you must achieve two goals: 1) confirm no unauthorized credit reports exist in your child's name, and 2) keep your child identity-theft free throughout childhood. Consumer laws and regulations make achieving your first goal relatively easy, but keeping your children safe gets complicated for reasons you'll see shortly.

Start by confirming with the three credit-reporting firms that no credit report exists in your child's name. Do that by sending a letter to each of the three companies requesting they conduct a manual search on your child's Social Security number. (See our Hack-Proof Action Guide for complete details.)

Usually the review discovers nothing unless you've added your child's name to one of your credit cards. If no credit files appear, no credit exists in your child's name—a good result. If you discover an unauthorized credit file in your child's name—a telltale sign of identity theft—things get complicated. Put a Security Freeze on your child's file immediately and investigate further.[3]

Keeping Your Kids Safe

Finding a long-term solution to keeping your child safe from identity theft poses some complications. If you're like us, you'd prefer a way to put a Security Freeze on your child's name and be done. Unfortunately, consumer credit laws and regulations have not kept pace with the identity-theft problem.

Less than half the states have laws in place to protect minors' credit. Some states allow a parent or guardian to create a credit report for a minor and then freeze it. Others will flag the minor's Social Security number to prevent credit from being issued. But no comprehensive approach yet exists.[4]

Guarding the Social

Parents should heed a few other cautions. Guard your child's Social Security number, and always question why someone needs it. Keep the card in your home, not in a purse or wallet, and shred any documents that include the number and other identifying information.[5]

Hack-Proof Action Step #11

☐ Request a search on your children's Social Security numbers at all three credit bureaus.

☐ Review your state's laws to determine the best way to protect your children from identity theft.

Completion date: __/__/____   Score: 5 points

For assistance on confirming your child's identity has not been stolen and finding what rules govern protection of children's identities in your state, turn to page 160 of the Action Guide.

12

How to Spot ATM Skimmers and Foil Identity Thieves

Full Tank, Empty Bank Account, and the Sting of Gas-Pump Skimmers

HACK REPORT: When Idahoan Debbie Davis stopped for gas one day at a local convenience store, she swiped her card at the pump, just like always. But when attempting to use her debit card a few days later, Davis discovered she had no money. The bank had frozen her account for "suspicious activity."

Unknown to the woman, a ring of thieves had rigged the pumps at her usual fill-up spot and six others throughout Idaho. They'd placed "skimmer" devices inside the pumps that illegally recorded people's names and card numbers and then exploited that stolen information to forge duplicate cards. To complete their scam, they'd fill a modified pickup truck with three-hundred gallons of fuel purchased with fraudulent bank cards and then sell the gas at half price.

In Davis's case, the thieves charged her debit card for $1,500 of fuel. Ultimately, federal and state agents in Idaho and California busted the skimming ring and charged seven people. "It was always at a truck stop," she told the *Idaho Statesman*.[1] "I couldn't understand how that could happen when I still had my card in my hand."

Rule #12: Know How to Spot a Skimmer Device, and Avoid Non-Bank ATMs

Most people who get their cash from machines know they should exercise caution when entering their PINs and withdrawing money; far fewer know how to watch for skimmer devices, a class of tools thieves secretly deploy to read and record your bank cards and then quickly drain your accounts.[2]

Now, with the advent of 3-D printers, thieves can create fake fronts to slip tightly over an existing ATM keypad or other self-payment kiosks. Once the skimmer is placed—sometimes even inside a payment machine—the crooks will record your card and PIN data, fashion new cards, or use the information for illegal purchases.[3]

Three Tips for Avoiding Skimmers

So knowing how to spot a skimmer will protect you from this fraud. Follow these guidelines: First, only use card-reading machines that you trust.[4] Bank ATMs are somewhat harder for thieves to rig compared to convenience stores. Second, always inspect a machine before starting. If the card slot appears flimsy or jiggles, stop. Any ATM with a wobbly, shaky part indicates tampering. Third, always cover the keypad when entering your number. Sometimes, crooks will install a camera with the skimmer to record you entering your PIN.[5]

Trust your instincts. If something feels "off" about an ATM or payment kiosk, don't use it. Let an employee know and find a more secure machine.

In a worst-case scenario, if you must use a sketchy machine, use a credit card rather than a debit card. Your credit-card liability stops at $50, while your personal responsibility for debit-card losses caps at $500.[6]

Skimmers and EMV Cards

You may wonder if skimmers work with new EMV chip-based cards. They don't, because these cards generate a temporary code each time you make a payment, and the entire process is encrypted. Recording the card wouldn't help the thieves. So you should always dip your card, and not swipe, at any payment machine that offers an option. EMV (which stands for Europay, MasterCard, and Visa) cards do improve security against skimming, but they don't offer protection against online fraud stemming from data breaches of companies that hold your credit card number.[7]

Knowing how to spot skimming will help hack-proof your life. But as we saw in this chapter's Hack Report, sometimes the fraudsters' skimmers are undetectable. Even if you do get hacked that way, though, you'll have a second line of defense. You'll see a problem right away when you get details of an unauthorized charge in a text or email alert—a good example of the power of the New Cybersecurity Rules working together to protect you.

Hack-Proof Action Step #12

☐ Understand how to inspect any ATM or payment kiosk for possible skimming fraud.

☐ Avoid using non-bank ATMs for withdrawing cash.

Completion date: __/__/____   Score: 5 points

For more information about your personal liability in any bank card or credit card fraud, turn to page 166 of the Action Guide.

PART III

Mindfulness

Stay Hack-Proofed
When Your Brain Says *Click!*

A key aspect of using the Internet involves one simple, physical action—clicking. For most of us, our first computer lesson involved learning to click. We clicked to open programs, edit files, and complete hundreds of other actions. Then email came along and we clicked to send messages. Finally, when computer scientists introduced the World Wide Web, we learned to click on links.

Clicking makes the Internet work. All the billions of pages on the global network connect through hyperlinks. When we run our computers or devices, we click or tap, often without thinking. So, just as we started this book, we now return to the click. The most important, most elemental aspect of our interconnected cyber world also poses the gravest threat to our security. We need to understand why we click and keep clicking, even to the point of danger.

Your Brain and Clicking

In 1954, scientists made a discovery about the brain and stimulation. They learned that rats would endlessly click a lever that electrically stimulated their brain's pleasure center. The rodents would continue to click up to seven hundred times an hour—even rejecting food and water—until death. Later, scientists concluded that stimulating a rat's brain released the chemical dopamine, which caused the creatures to want even more pleasure, renewing their desire for more self-stimulation. Humans are similar.

We know that dopamine is critical to brain function. Once released, this neurotransmitter causes us to want, desire, and seek out. It also makes us curious about ideas and fuels our search for information.[1]

Just a few years before the rat and dopamine studies, Zenith introduced a magical new way to change the channel on the television without leaving your couch—an idea first patented by the inventor Nikola Tesla. Zenith's realization of Tesla's over-the-air, radio-frequency controller became the world's first remote-control TV clicker.[2] And with it, Zenith launched a new era of human behavior: endlessly clicking to exhaustion or sleep. You see, the channel changer became the world's first rapid dopamine delivery system, and humans learned, just like the rats, that we love to click, too.

Google and the Click

Have you ever gone on Google to search for one thing and found yourself thirty minutes later still clicking away on other things? That repeated clicking for more information is the dopamine working on you. Each tap of the finger, each new bit of data, and each new image on the screen delivers more dopamine and renews the desire to click again. (If you've ever heard of "Internet addiction," you may better understand the malady when you know that there's a chemical reaction—clicking releases dopamine.)

Google search results, and their invitation to click, create a powerful distraction that University of Michigan psychology Professor Kent Berridge says can lead to irrational, excessive wants we'd be better off without. "We find ourselves letting one Google search lead to another. ... As long as you sit there, the consumption renews the appetite."[3]

Click Roulette

Clicking on links reinforces an emotional state of seeking. Our communication devices feed the same drive, too: The unpredictable stream of texts, emails, and notifications that pour into our computers and smartphones intrigue and excite us.

Each ring, each buzz, each ding delivers a sensory stimulation that signals to us that someone or something wants our attention. Our devices make us curious and then keep renewing that feeling. And all that excitation takes a toll.

Each alert we receive taxes our mental battery. The distraction of multitasking fractures our defenses. Finally, fatigue enters. We become less guarded and less analytical about potential attacks.[3] One scary-sounding subject line in an official-looking email and we click before we evaluate the message.

Technology primes our brains to click. In our distracted state, the act of opening our email practically becomes a game of click roulette. The more devices you use, the more clicking opportunities you face, and the greater the chance you will accidentally click badly and invite disaster.

Consider how this works to the hacker's advantage: In the 1970s, most people's chief communication device was a phone they shared with their family. By 1993, there were two million PCs connected to the Internet.[4] By 2016, that number had jumped to four billion devices worldwide.[5] The average American household owns more than five connected devices, and each one provides us a chance to click.[6]

Mindfulness and the Unrelenting Attack

Remember, spammers blast out more than ninety-four billion dangerous emails every day[7] and the hackers produce more than eight hundred thousand new malware programs daily.[8] Anyone with an email address faces an unrelenting, if not always visible, attack. To meet this challenge to our cybersecurity, our brains must be vigilant but controlled. So how do we reshape our day-to-day cybersecurity practices to keep alert and safe without going crazy?

In some ways, the answer lies in the behaviors we first learned to safely operate a car.

When driving a car, ideally you operate in a state of relaxed alertness ready to respond to sudden changes on the road. Safe use of the Internet requires the same type of alertness. Similarly, fighter pilots describe this type of situational awareness with the acronym "OODA," which stands for observation, orientation, decision, and action.[9] Productivity experts and psychologists describe this optimal state as "flow."[10] Zen masters prefer the term "mindfulness."[11]

Shortly after we finished our initial research for this book, Google released a survey that examined the practices of security experts and ordinary Internet users. Not surprisingly, Google researchers arrived at many of the same conclusions we did. They, too, emphasized the importance of how we view our daily cybersecurity practices and described that state using the word mindfulness.[12] We like mindfulness, because the word relates to how you engage the Internet moment to moment and gives you a framework for how to stay safe, especially after you've adopted all the New Cybersecurity Rules.

So, now we're going to show you how to complete the process of hack-proofing your life. In these final chapters, we'll introduce you to a set of behaviors and security actions that will keep you strong and secure into the future. You'll learn how to follow the same key steps that top security experts take to keep hackers out of their computers, and you'll understand how to avoid ever paying extortion to cyber blackmailers. We'll show you how to stop playing click roulette by practicing the Ten-Second EMAIL Rule to unmask any suspicious attacks that enter your inbox. Finally, we'll answer a very common question we hear about LifeLock and explain why we think you should *never* outsource your personal cybersecurity to any company that promises to monitor your digital life against identity theft and cyber attacks.

When you follow the final set of New Cybersecurity Rules, you'll have closed your cybersecurity gap and boosted your Cybersecurity Score to the greatest extent possible—you'll have hack-proofed your life. Now, let's finish.

13

The One Software Program
You Must Know Well

Scareware Virus Strikes Terror in People Unfamiliar with Antivirus Software

HACK REPORT: Blogger and social media business consultant Stevie Wilson was working on her computer one day when a pop-up alert grabbed her attention. It said: "You just downloaded a virus."

"That is a phrase that puts terror into the heart of anybody," Wilson says in a Vimeo video.[1] Little did she know that she'd unwittingly triggered a clever attack known as "scareware." The pop-up, from a company called "Personal Antivirus," looked very official. The window urged her to click a link so the antivirus software could run a full scan of her machine to detect other bugs. "I fell for this because it was so generic-looking. It didn't have a lot of bells and whistles."

Wilson clicked and waited. Bad news. A window delivered the message: Her computer was infected with dozens of Trojan horses, worms, and viruses. The alert advised Wilson she needed to pay for an upgrade to her antivirus program, which she immediately did, completing the second step of the scareware scam. Now the hackers had her credit-card number, too.

After downloading the "upgraded antivirus software," Wilson rebooted her computer. It was dead. "I lost photos, videos, parts of stories," she said. "So much stuff." Wilson had to wipe her hard drive clean and reinstall everything. "These people created a program that says you have a virus—which is a lie—so you will download something," she says. "You run a scan, so they have access into your computer, and then they're charging you for the download they're purporting is actually a fix, which it isn't. It's actually going in and screwing up your computer even worse."

Wilson admits she panicked in the moment and acted without thinking. "That's the wrong reaction to have. You need to stay calm, because the more you panic, the worse it's going to get. Staying calm is important. I'm trying to learn how to do that."

Rule #13: Install Antivirus Software Now

Imagine opening your computer and seeing this message on the screen:

"I'M THE CREEPER. CATCH ME IF YOU CAN."

Sounds ominous, right? It actually happened in the 1970s. Creeper was the first computer virus, an experiment that immediately led to the release of another program, called Reaper, which sniffed out Creeper and neutralized it. Reaper was the first antivirus.[2]

At the time, the computer scientists didn't understand the full significance of the event, but their Creeper and Reaper experiments would later spawn an entire computer-protection industry. Once the "black hat" programmers learned to harness the computer for crime and mischief, everyone needed protection. Our computer lexicon grew to include words such as bug, worm, virus, and even Trojan, each a metaphor for malware capable of carrying out real harm: leaked data, erased files, and ruined computers.

Now, more than thirty years into the personal computer revolution, fear, confusion, and helplessness still reign over catching infections. Unprotected Internet surfing remains dangerous. One recent study by security firm Kaspersky identified 121 million virulent programs in the Internet "wild."[3] What does that mean? Well, one visit to an infected website and you could suffer a "drive-by download," a malicious program that quietly enters your computer and commences a range of activities that lead to identity theft, data breaches, or ransomware extortion. Your computer could be secretly recording personal data and contacts, or connecting to a global network of spam-sending robots.[4] Nasty stuff.

The Creeper-Reaper experiments pointed to the future. We now face a malware arms race that seems to grow in reach and sophistication each passing day. So, in order to hack-proof your life, you need to install a good antivirus software program on your computers and devices.

Yes, We Mean You!

How could it be that people still ask whether they really need protection on their computers? Hopefully, not you. But many Windows and Apple computer owners still believe they don't need antivirus software, and experts estimate nearly 25 percent of machines don't have the protection program.[5] That means those computers are five times more likely to get infected. Yes, no virus detection software is perfect—an impossible expectation—but the programs will catch the majority of threats, lessening your chances of getting a virus or other malware.

Top Reasons You Need Protection

When researchers examine why people don't protect their computers, they see a tangle of problems, misconceptions, and a lack of information. If this includes you, let's look at three reasons for adding antivirus detection:

1. **Provides insurance:** Some people used to view antivirus software as a waste of money. Skeptics saw the antivirus industry as a "protection racket" that preyed on the public's fears—arguably true in some past cases, but no longer. Now, savvy computer users regard antivirus software as the equivalent of an insurance policy. For an annual subscription from

around $40 to $60, a good program will run quietly in the background and scan your computer for invaders. The small cost seems like a fair trade to avoid the fear, stress, and lost productivity that accompany a crippling malware infection.

2. **Eliminates scareware:** If you run virus detection software, you should never fall victim to the "fake antivirus scam" we saw working in this chapter's Hack Report. When you operate antivirus software on your machine, you'll actually be familiar with the program and how it works. You'll know a persistent pop-up telling you've been infected is suspicious, right? You'll just launch your own antivirus program to investigate.

3. **Protects your family:** Another sensible reason to install antivirus software involves other people who share your computer, especially young kids and unsophisticated computer users (you know who they are). Kids take to computers with ease, but they're still naïve and uninformed. One quick search and a click for a Minecraft or Club Penguin shortcut, and your computer could be in danger: Who knows what they'll click and download when you're not watching?

Take Action

If you don't already have antivirus software running on your machine, you'll want to add it now.[6] Even though the program can protect you from many cybersecurity threats, it won't shield you from everything, and you must remain vigilant about your security.

Just don't become paranoid. Yes, hackers pose a real risk, and a hack-proofed life requires antivirus software. But if you follow the New Cybersecurity Rules and run an updated antivirus program on your computer and devices, you'll be fine. "Updated" is the operative word, as you'll see next.

Hack-Proof Action Step #13

☐ Install and update antivirus software on your computers and devices.

Completion date: __/__/____   Score: 5 points

Consult our Action Guide on page 167 for details on choosing antivirus programs and directions on how to control who downloads files on your shared computer.

What Security Experts ALWAYS Do and Why You Should Do the Same

One Blogger's Solution
to Chronically Unsafe Software—Just Uninstall

HACK REPORT: Few people research cybersecurity issues in greater detail than Brian Krebs. Industry experts consider his *Krebs on Security* blog a must-read. If a new threat emerges somewhere on the Internet, chances are he reported the incident first, or soon thereafter.

One topic the former *Washington Post* writer follows closely is buggy and insecure software, and the need to update these programs immediately with a security patch. One big cybersecurity problem we face involves hackers exploiting weaknesses they discover in popular programs produced by Adobe, Apple, Google, Microsoft, and Oracle.

Out-of-date software presents an easy target for hackers. The holes in the programs allow them to quietly monitor your computer use and plant viruses and malicious software to aid their frauds. Security experts call these software openings "zero-day exploits" because hackers attack the insecure program before the vendor discovers the problem.

Krebs routinely reports which companies have released new security patches to close the holes. It's very much a cat-and-mouse game between the software developers and the hackers. So, it was not surprising when Krebs one day announced that he'd completed an unusual experiment. He had grown weary of the never-ending series of patches issued for the Adobe Flash Player, the plugin and software that plays videos and special effects in a web browser.[1]

"Browser plugins are favorite targets for malware and miscreants because they are generally full of unpatched or undocumented security holes that cyber crooks can use to seize complete control over vulnerable systems," Krebs wrote. And every time Adobe issues a new update for Flash, the hackers quickly find a new way to exploit the software. He announced that he'd found a new approach to the "patch madness" annoyance.

"I've spent the better part of the last month running a little experiment to see how much I would miss Adobe's buggy and insecure Flash Player software if I removed it from my systems altogether," he said. "Turns out, not so much." Krebs encountered only two instances where Adobe Flash was necessary for something he wanted to view. In those cases, he enabled Flash to play in a browser and then later disabled the program.

As we'll see with this chapter, maintaining your hack-proof life demands keeping your software updated at all times. But as Krebs points out, sometimes you can get along just fine without some programs.

Rule #14: Always Update Your Software and Uninstall Unsafe Programs

As we've seen, building a hack-proofed life involves taking a series of discrete, easy-to-complete steps. None of them involves rocket science, and each move boosts your cybersecurity. Some New Cybersecurity Rules require one-time actions: You put them in place and continuously benefit, such as putting alerts on your financial accounts. But other actions must become part of your routine online behavior. In this chapter, we address two behaviors you absolutely must adopt: updating software and uninstalling unsafe and unused programs.

Nine out of ten security experts will tell you that strong security always requires that you update your software—no excuses.[2] The updates, also called patches, close known security holes, the places where hackers quietly slip malicious booby traps onto your computer or device. Yet people commonly overlook or knowingly avoid software updates.

We know from experience. Sadly, many complicated reasons exist for why an estimated 40 percent of computer users don't accept critical software patches in a safe, timely manner.[3] Worse, security experts say that 75 to 80 percent of the time they see a computer hack, the problem traces to outdated software, and often the special-use programs Adobe Acrobat Reader, Adobe Flash, Java, and Internet browsers (Chrome, Firefox, Internet Explorer).[4]

The Outdated Software Risk

Experts say the hack happens this way: If you visit an infected website, follow a spam email link, or click a deceptive pop-up window, the hackers' programs can detect unplugged software holes on your computer and drop damaging programs on your machine. The malicious code could be anything from spyware recording your usernames and passwords, to a robot secretly sending spam emails from your computer, to ransomware kidnapping your computer files in return for payment.[5]

Few of us appreciate the serious consequences of running outdated software. We all want security, and our software and hardware, no matter how good, eventually need updates to fix bugs and patch holes. But often we don't do that because of four common concerns.

First, software makers tell us to download newer versions, but the update just adds a feature that we don't want. We like the way the program runs now and we ignore the request. Second, a poorly written update announcement makes no sense, so we do nothing. Third, downloading some software in the past slowed our computer or added toolbars or plugins we didn't want, so we do nothing. And fourth, we fear that the update itself will contain a bug and cause our computer to stop working.[6] We definitely do nothing.

Our experiences and reasons for avoiding software updates make sense, but they don't erase the important reality: running your computer on unpatched software invites trouble. We need to respect the seriousness of software updates and change our mindset and behavior about our personal cybersecurity. Only then can we have peace of mind about our personal cybersecurity—a chief benefit of a hack-proofed life.

Three Software Update Myths

Let's look at three mental roadblocks that prevent us from keeping our software current:

1. **Junkware download:** Don't confuse downloading a software *update* with a past bad experience of an *initial* software download—two different things often conflated.[7] Our behavior based on past experiences makes sense. Many of us bear scars we associate with a troublesome *software download*. Who hasn't added software that put a new, messy toolbar, icon, or some other annoyance on our browser? We hate it.

   But a *software update* didn't cause those experiences. Don't mix up downloading a game, a plugin, or a video player with adding a security patch. No reputable company will add uninvited junkware during the update process.

2. **Beware of on-screen demands:** Hackers have inserted themselves directly into the software update challenge. They've created malicious programs (often fake antivirus software) specifically designed to frighten us into downloading their malware.[8] They know that if we face repeated, urgent demands to update software, many of us will succumb to their scam, and even pay for fraudulent

over-the-phone technical support in the process—a double insult. Don't let them manipulate you.

An easy solution exists. Never respond to pestering on-screen requests—a likely scam. If in doubt, simply visit the software-maker's website or Google its name and the word "update" to investigate.

3. **The "restart your computer" myth:** Inevitably, adding a critical software patch coincides with being totally busy. Many computer users wrongly believe that accepting an update means you must stop working while your computer restarts. Not true. So don't let this myth hurt you. Nearly all good software programs give you the option to download the update in the background, allowing you to continue working, and then finish the update later by restarting your computer.[9] Just read the update screen.

The Automatic Update Solution

Now you can see that no good reason exists to avoid updating your software. Tracking all your software programs sounds daunting, especially since active computer users have at least twenty to fifty programs. Thankfully, some software makers allow you to get automatic updates, or update notifications, to their programs. For Mac, click the Apple icon in the toolbar, select System Preferences, and then App Store. From there, you can customize when to receive notifications about your operating system and app updates.[10] If you run Microsoft Office, go to Help and select Check for Updates. You'll see options for Microsoft AutoUpdates. For Windows, click the Start button or go to Control Panel (or Settings) and then select Windows Update (or Update & Security). The Change Settings pane will show how to schedule and install updates, including Microsoft Office.[11]

If you set your computer to actively monitor for software updates, you'll have achieved one of the easiest ways to improve your security. You'll be alerted to act.

Keeping your web browsers updated takes little effort, too. Each time you close them, they automatically update. Just don't keep browsers open for weeks or you will miss important security updates.

Uninstall Unsafe and Old Programs

This rule's second part involves old or chronically unsecure programs. As we saw in the Hack Report, programs such as Adobe Flash Player have become security headaches in constant need of new patches. Oracle's Java faces similar problems.[12] The developers of these programs didn't anticipate the possibility that hackers would constantly seek new ways to invade their programs. Now, years later, many computers hold these unsafe programs. Unless you need them, we recommend you uninstall or disable Flash and Java.

Many people face a different problem. Older software programs, such as Microsoft's Windows XP and Windows Vista operating systems and Apple's QuickTime program for Windows, no longer receive support from their makers.[13] The companies have developed newer, better programs and have stopped issuing security updates. Remember, hackers can detect these older programs and exploit their security holes to your detriment. You must uninstall them.

Additionally, programs you've downloaded in the past, tried out once or twice, and then never used also present problems. You should review all the software on your computers and devices and uninstall the ones you no longer use. They present potential problems.

Update and Uninstall

If you clean your computer of unsafe and old software, set your desktop and laptop computers to automatically update software, and embrace routinely updating your smartphone and tablet software, you'll enjoy stronger security. Your state of being hack-proofed will be renewed with each update.

Hack-Proof Action Step #14

☐ Always update your software when prompted and set your programs to automatically download current versions, if that's an option.

☐ Uninstall or disable unsafe software and programs you don't use.

☐ Regularly update your smartphone and tablet software and apps.

Completion date: __/__/____   Score: 5 points

See our Action Guide on page 171 for more details on uninstalling and disabling programs, plus other software guidance.

How to Guarantee You Never Pay Extortion to Cyber Thieves

The Tale of Two Companies Identically Phished

HACK REPORT: Two small companies suffered identical cyber-extortion plots. One side-stepped the consequences of the ransomware attack, but the other company could not evade the hacker's demands.

At the first company, based in Hermitage, Tennessee, an employee received an email from PayPal. The message announced that someone had paid him money and he just needed to click a link to learn who. The email looked perfectly legitimate, the company's network manager Eric Young told National Public Radio (NPR). "It had the exact background of PayPal."[1]

So Young's colleague clicked. In seconds, the computer screen announced the arrival of CryptoWall 2.0, a type of ransomware that digitally kidnaps a computer's files, locks them behind super-strong encryption, and holds them for ransom. A cyber mugging.

The CryptoWall virus informed the firm it had seventy-two hours to pay up. As Young investigated, the ransomware virus spread to other machines on his network. Before long, the malware had encrypted the company's crucial database. "We lost everything we had built for fourteen years."

Fortunately, Young practiced good cybersecurity. He didn't have to worry about whether the hackers would actually return the files in exchange for ransom. He had backup copies of the firm's data. While cleaning the infected computers consumed a lot of time, the company did not submit to the hacker's extortion.

At the second company, based in Colorado Springs, Colorado, a similar scenario unfolded. Except no one called the network manager for help—instead, someone rang the police and an officer responded immediately. But by the time he arrived, the firm had already decided the police could do nothing and the only option was to pay the $750 ransom. No backup files existed to restore their computers to their pre-encrypted state.

So we see identical crimes with two different outcomes. One company survived by protecting its data with a separate backup (though certainly its leaders suffered serious stress knowing fourteen years of intellectual property and data hung in the balance). The second organization, lacking the only surefire solution to snubbing the blackmailers—a backup—yielded to the criminals.

Were they right? The Department of Homeland Security says don't pay hackers. However, experts told NPR decrypting the files would be impossible and noted that a Tennessee sheriff's office had recently paid phishers for its records. So if you have no backup, you have no defense against ransomware.

Rule #15: Back Up Your Files So You Never Pay Ransomware Extortion

Our digital life is more than just our personal data, it's also our digital possessions.

Let's put aside cybersecurity for one moment: Imagine walking through a typical modern home from the early 1990s. Nearly every room contains some physical item that now, more than twenty-five years later, has been absorbed by the digital revolution. Think about it: tapes, albums, CDs—all software and computer bytes now. Home movies, letter folders, family albums, filing cabinets, and recipe boxes—the same. Books, journals, notebooks, calendars, diaries, and medical and tax records—all digital. Even TV, movies, and radio stream to our computers and devices.

So, computers not only contain our digital lives, they also hold much of our former physical possessions. No wonder people and companies readily succumb to extortion. If you don't back up your files, whether deeply sentimental or critical to your business, you have no choice. When blackmail strikes, you must pay.

Hackers increasingly deploy the favored, profitable ransomware programs—a nearly perfect crime. The victims volunteer themselves with one errant click and the crooks pressure victims to act quickly or see the ransom double. Victims, often embarrassed, pay the money in the untraceable digital currency called Bitcoin. Security experts estimated a recent year of encryption attacks netted cyber criminals $325 million in ransom from more than four hundred and forty thousand victims.[2] That's more than twelve-hundred victims per day paying $500 to $750 each to get their computer files decrypted and released for continued use. The police have little power to investigate and solve these borderless cyber crimes. Nice, huh?

Rule of Three: Never Pay Ransomware

Now recall the first page of *Hack-Proof Your Life Now!* We told you the story of our very smart, attentive colleague who clicked on a ransomware link. He escaped catastrophe because we had backed up his computer, but it took nearly two days to get his machine running again, and he still lost a small amount of data. Don't let that happen to you—follow the "rule of three" for strong security.[3]

The rule says you need three copies of your files: one on your computer or device; the other stored in the "cloud," meaning the files sit on an Internet-connected server that syncs with your computer; and the third stored in a physical backup device, usually an external computer drive.

Backing up your data makes good sense for two reasons, and not just because of hackers. First, you want to possess safe, duplicate copies of your files purely for technical reasons and acts of God: A backup protects you against computer failure (hard-drive crash), theft, and natural or human-caused disasters. Researchers claim everyone will ultimately suffer at least one of these losses. Remember, power surges, burglaries, lightning strikes, hurricanes, earthquakes, and tornadoes do happen.

Second, if you fall for ransomware, you won't need to pay the hackers. If you back up your files in multiple places, you'll never suffer blackmail or catastrophic data loss because you'll be hack-proofed.

Help! I Clicked!

People often ask us, "What should I do if I get infected with ransomware?" First, immediately disconnect your computer from any network to prevent the infection from spreading to other computers. Second, get a technician who can help you delete the ransomware from your machine and assist in possible recovery of your files.[4] The cleaning will take time and money.

If you have no backup and must regain your files, you'll need to obtain a bitcoin wallet to pay the ransom.

Backing up your files remains your best defense against the phisher's dreaded ransomware. But we don't think that will happen to you once you hack-proof your life and learn the all-important Ten-Second EMAIL Rule starting in the next chapter.

Hack-Proof Action Step #15

☐ Back up your data on ALL your devices to at least two locations—the cloud and a physical device.

Completion date: __/__/____   Score: 5 points

For information on products and services that will help you achieve the rule of three and back up your computer and devices, plus directions for buying bitcoins, turn to page 178 in the Action Guide.

Hackers Never Sleep: Spot the Phisher's Mind Tricks

(Ten-Second EMAIL Rule, Part One)

Spoofed Email from White House Advisor Opens Door for Hackers

HACK REPORT: Sometimes the simplest email request can trigger turmoil. Consider the wife of a White House official who received an innocuous-sounding email from her husband: "Hey, Honey, do you have the password for our joint Xfinity account? I lost it."

The spoofed email message seemed to come from John P. Holdren, assistant to President Obama and director of the White House Office of Science and Technology Policy. According to the technology blog *Motherboard*, Holdren's wife responded by sending the password to their Xfinity phone and Internet service.[1] Then trouble started—she actually sent the password to hackers.

In one second, the Holdrens became the latest victims of "Crackas with Attitude," political hackers supporting Palestinian statehood, whose previous exploits had snared the personal email accounts of the nation's top super-spies, CIA Director John Brennan and Director of National Intelligence James Clapper, plus other top White House officials.

The episode reveals a new truth about public life: Scrutiny comes from hackers, too. To reach public officials, hackers look to exploit officials' family members and associates as possible weak links. Sometimes a short fraudulent email message can dislodge one bit of data needed to launch a scam—as the hackers did with Holdren's wife. They described to *Motherboard* what is known as a "spear-phishing" attack, a ruse aimed at a single person or group. (A typical phishing effort scams any victim who clicks a link the fraudsters emailed to thousands or millions of people.)

Once hackers had the Holdrens' Xfinity password, they entered the family's phone system and completed a prank they'd pulled before, redirecting the victim's phone to ring at the offices of the Free Palestine Movement.

The scam demonstrates the difficult challenge we all face with phishing. Could Holdren's wife have stopped the cyber assault? Maybe. She received a spoofed email, a common approach used by hackers in which the email message has a forged header that appeared to come from her husband. But spoofed emails can be unmasked. It takes just ten seconds. As we'll see in this chapter and the next, knowing how to uncover the true origin of an email will boost your defenses against phishing.

Rule #16: Examine Email Messages to Determine the True Sender

Now it's time to learn how to spot a phisher's click bait, one of the most important skills you'll learn in *Hack-Proof Your Life Now!* You see, every single day you face a phishing risk, even when you run good antivirus software, keep your software up to date, and back up your files. The hackers never sleep: Their email servers pump out nearly one billion malware-loaded emails around the clock.[2]

So, in order to have a hack-proofed life, we need a mental framework for staying alert and mindful while we use the Internet. Meet our Ten-Second EMAIL Rule: EMAIL stands for Examine Message And Inspect Links.

EMAIL is our easy-to-remember two-part defense system. Once you learn the rule, EMAIL will serve as your mental tool to spot and dismiss the scammers, phishers, and fraudsters. You won't lose your money or identity to hackers.

The Phishing Threat

Currently, phishing is the leading strategy for fraudsters. Experts believe this will continue, because the scam's versatile and adaptable nature makes it profitable and difficult to stop. Sending a legitimate-looking email, often from a well-known bank, brand, or social media company, remains the phisher's most compelling lure.

Hackers want you to click. As we know, one finger tap on a malicious link can produce ugly consequences, such as infecting your computer with spyware to record your actions, tricking you to reveal your personal data through a well-forged website, and even virtual kidnapping of your computer files.

Thankfully, you never see most phishing emails. They get blocked upstream by your email provider's spam filters and security systems and never reach your inbox. But the spam never stops.

The hackers snare both neophytes and sophisticated Internet users alike. Their oldest tricks keep finding new, profitable victims. Sadly, the phishers' malicious software continues to change form. As soon as experts shut down one type of attack, the hackers quickly return with a new variant of malicious spam—an estimated eight hundred thousand new malware programs are released into the Internet wild daily.[3]

You can see why the phishing crime wave appears unstoppable. Experts say the hackers' spam attacks reach half of all Internet users each day with at least a single malicious email.[4] They might hook your Aunt Bea one moment, your boss the next, and then even a high-ranking government official. Hackers rarely discriminate.

Phisher's Subject-Line Hook

The phishing emails that slip through the global spam filters arrive uninvited in our inbox and with malice embedded in their links. A successful phisher manipulates our emotions and induces panic and impulsive action. Psychologists call this "social engineering," a crime of the mind designed to trick you into doing things you'd rather not. The scam starts with the subject line. Phishers hook you with their email titles.[5]

Originally, in their earliest and simplest forms—forged bank or credit-card notifications—phishing emails featured alarming subject lines such as Warning, Violation, Security Alert, Account Locked, or even a stunning Account Closed. The subject lines worked well and continue to hook victims today.

But hackers' tactics change. A newer generation of phishing delivers a blander tone with seemingly legitimate, even intriguing titles such as:

- Invitation to Connect on LinkedIn

- Mail Delivery Failed: Return Message to Sender

- Facebook Support Sent You a Message

- Incoming Payment Received

- Your Statement Is Available Online

- Password Reset Notification

- Unauthorized Access Denied

As you can see, any one would pique curiosity. But how can you sniff out and separate the malicious, interloping emails from the legitimate ones? The first half of the Ten-Second EMAIL Rule—Examine Message—gets you started. First, scrutinize an email message's subject line and content from an emotional and psychological perspective: *What are they saying? What do they want me to do and why? Does it really make sense?* You can best achieve our call to "Examine Message" by seeing if the email passes these quick tests:

True sender test: Determine the real sender. Phishers always mask their true identity by forging the sender's display name, an easy task.[6]

On the surface, an email's "from line" may show a company's name such as "American Express." Or it might display an actual address, such as Service@AmericanExpress.com. Don't trust it. Unmasking a forgery usually takes just a second. Some email programs do the work when you open the email. The fake address will appear right next to the display name. With some other programs, just hover your mouse pointer over the name. You'll see a balloon or small box that will show the real address. Does it seem right, such as <Service@ AmericanExpress.com>? Or does it arouse suspicion, such as this one: American Express <ihceq@twelve.co.id>? If the address seems less than straightforward, act with caution and examine other parts of the message.

Greetings test: Check the salutation for errors. A poor phishing email will fail this test immediately, especially if the greeting field is blank or just includes your email address. No serious business email would address you that way. However, with so much of our personal data now for sale on the black market, phishers can craft very convincing emails. In the past, you might have been addressed as "Dear Valued Customer." Now, a fraudulent email could arrive fully personalized with our name and address, among other details. Stay on guard. Keep examining the message.

Grammar test: Look for misspelled words or poor grammar. Hackers certainly know computers, but their emails often contain errors you'd never expect from a legitimate sender.

Signature test: Determine if a real person with contact information signed the email. Does the signature name match the email address behind the sender's display name? Anything vague or unclear about the signature also hints at fraud.

Attachments test: An email with an attachment signals potential danger. Never click to open an unsolicited attachment. What presents itself as a possible résumé, receipt, or payment could be an .exe file that plants a virus or seizes your computer for ransom.

If an email fails any of these tests, simply delete it and move on.[7] Don't waste your time with hackers. But if you still harbor doubt, follow part two of the Ten-Second EMAIL Rule, which shows you how to inspect links.

Hack-Proof Action Step #16

☐ Learn how to unmask an email's true sender on the display-name line.

☐ Understand how to examine an email message for the key signs of fraud.

Completion date: __/__/____   Score: 5 points

For more details on examining an email to learn its true sender, insights on anti-phishing browser plugins, and text and telephone phishing exploits, turn to page 181 of the Action Guide.

17

The Phisher's Seduction: He Hooks with the Link

(Ten-Second EMAIL Rule, Part Two)

Shock, Panic, Disaster—
Phishing Link Breaks Journalist's Deadline

HACK REPORT: British writer Jane Corbin hurried to complete a documentary; her deadline was less than an hour away. Suddenly, she spotted an alarming email from Yahoo. The message told Corbin to confirm her account details immediately or Yahoo would close the account. "It looked authentic—the graphics, the text, the disclaimer at the bottom were identical to the ones used by Yahoo—even some of the details about my account were accurate," she recounted for the *Daily Mail*.[1]

Corbin panicked and clicked a link that took her to a fake Yahoo website. "So I did what I never should have done," she said. "I filled in all the boxes, including my password, and pressed the enter key. Within a minute my screen went blank, my electronic lifeline was severed, and the nightmare began."

Almost immediately, more than a thousand people on her contact list received a forged email from Corbin, saying she had been robbed while out of the country and needed money fast. Corbin had suffered a classic phishing attack and handed her personal data to the hackers. Now she was locked out of her computer and forced to close all her banking accounts as a precaution. It would be five days before Corbin regained her email account and new bank and credit cards.

If Corbin had taken ten seconds to closely examine the links in that forged Yahoo message, she could have avoided the stress, embarrassment, and lost time that results from a hack. Anyone can learn to spot a phishing email's bogus links.

Rule #17: Inspect Links to Confirm the Phisher's Fraud

We opened our book noting that trouble on the Internet always starts with a simple click. Now we're going to finish our journey together by showing you how to scrutinize the click's dangerous suitor—the link.

As we've seen, phishers have improved their black craft; their fraudulent emails now often appear as near-replicas of famous brands such as Apple, Bank of America, and LinkedIn. Everything about the message may appear correct, but hidden behind the email's clickable button or text is a treacherous hyperlink. So you must learn to inspect links—a critical skill to hack-proofing your life.

You just learned in the prior chapter how to unmask the true sender of an email and spot the clear signs of a phishing attack—the first part of our Ten-Second EMAIL RULE. Now we will teach you the second part.

You need to know how to identify malicious links, the actual digital hook phishers use to catch victims. In this moment-of-truth showdown between you and the hacker, he hopes your fear, your outrage, or your curiosity will cause you to surrender to his deception and click without thinking. And he offers clear, easy instructions.

You see, the phisher's call to action mimics the same instructions we read every day: Click Here, Update Now, Log In, Register, or anything that urges you to take action by clicking. Phishers do this well, and people fall into the trap because they click too quickly. That's why we must maintain caution and skepticism as we complete the Ten-Second EMAIL Rule and quickly discover any link's true destination.

Three Types of Hyperlinks

It takes just a second to spot the phisher's fake link if you know how and where to look. Remember, the hacker wants you to click and his links will appear legitimate.

1. **Typed link:** You've seen this in many places. It looks similar to a web address you see in your browser, such as http://www.AmericanExpress.com/loginupdate.

2. **Hyperlink:** This one is written in the Hyper Text Markup Language (HTML), the computer code that displays web and email pages and makes them interactive. A common HTML link is underlined and blue and says: Click Here.

3. **Clickable button or image:** Phishing emails may also contain hyperlinked buttons or images. Similar to an HTML link, a clickable button includes call-to-action text such as Log In or Update.

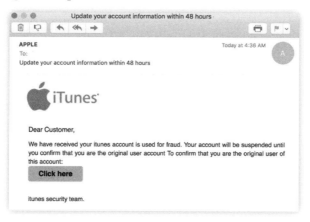

Now it's time to spot the fraud by using the second half of the Ten-Second EMAIL Rule—Inspect Link. Similar to the first part of the rule, just rest your mouse pointer directly over a suspicious link and see its true destination in the small balloon.[2] In the following example, you can see how the PayPal link looks completely official. But the balloon just below the pointer shows the alarming truth: a hacker's website obscured by its numeric IP address but cleverly including the name "paypal" at the end. Never click if you have the slightest concern.

Now you've learned the simple way to inspect any suspicious link. "Inspect Links" will always provide insights to the question: Is this a legitimate email?

Hack-Proof Confirmation

You're almost totally hack-proofed now. But for good measure, let's review a few more things about phishing emails:

Consider the sender: Remember, no legitimate bank or credit-card company will urgently email you, unprompted, and tell you to log in to your account.[3] Phishers don't want you to know this because it undermines their effective attacks. Similarly, you should never give anyone contacting you by email your personal information, credit-card numbers, or usernames and passwords. And if you receive similar uninitiated requests over the phone, refuse them and contact the company on your own.

No attachments: Remember, clicking attachments, just like links, can put dangerous malware on your computer or launch ransomware. Never open an unsolicited attachment.

Spotting secure websites: When you're inspecting a link, if its actual destination is a legitimate e-commerce or banking site, the web address will start with "https" like the Amazon example below. The "s" indicates the website has high security and privacy. You'll also see a padlock icon on the address line when you visit the website. Both signs indicate a secure website.[4]

Stay Calm and EMAIL

Security experts say most people can't spot a sophisticated phishing attack. But now you've learned the Ten-Second EMAIL Rule: You know how to spot trouble with our easy-to-remember framework for sniffing out and deleting any phisher's dangerous email. Every time you view a suspicious message, you'll think EMAIL: *Examine the Message to uncover the sender And Inspect the Links to confirm who sent it.* Practice this rule every day—repeat it as your mantra when checking email, because you never know when a phisher will enter your inbox.

This brings us nearly to the end of our mission to boost your cybersecurity and hack-proof your life. Now you know the New Cybersecurity Rules. The rest is up to you: Reduce the threat of hackers by being more secret in how you organize your finances; assume an omniscient role in your financial life as a critical backstop and defense against suffering fraud; and practice a daily mindfulness around the must-do security practices for your computers and devices. When you put Secrecy, Omniscience, and Mindfulness together, you know how to hack-proof your life.

We offer you our best wishes and encouragement: Stay Calm and EMAIL!

Hack-Proof Action Step #17

☐ Know how to inspect links in suspicious emails to determine if they're real or fraudulent.

☐ Recognize the danger of opening any unsolicited email attachment.

Completion date: __/__/____   Score: 5 points

See page 183 of our Action Guide for additional details on handling dangerous links on your mobile devices.

18

LifeLock and the Question: Whom Should You Trust to Protect Your Identity?

(Psst, Look in the Mirror.)

LifeLock Pays $100 Million Fine— FTC Cautions Consumers

HACK REPORT: When Sonny Ebarle joined LifeLock in 2012, he only wanted to keep himself and his family safe from the modern perils of credit fraud and identity theft.

LifeLock seemed the perfect solution. The company's advertising promised "comprehensive identity theft protection" that would keep people notified "up to the minute" if any thief tried to illegally obtain credit in a member's name. The service even offered a LifeLock Junior account for minor children, promoted as "relentless protection for your kids and peace of mind for you."

LifeLock's promises sounded good. For about $40 a month, Ebarle signed up with his wife and their two minor children.

Some time after joining, he noticed odd and suspicious activity around his family's credit files. Ebarle hadn't heard from LifeLock, though, and wondered why he wasn't getting the protection services and alerts promised by the company.

When Ebarle contacted LifeLock, he learned that the firm wasn't monitoring his wife's and children's accounts even though he'd been paying for family coverage. Quite a surprise. But that revelation would be the first of many for Ebarle, who soon would become the lead plaintiff in a class-action lawsuit against LifeLock alleging fraud.[1] Along the way, he would learn more about LifeLock, including:

- **LifeLock's fraud alert system had been declared illegal.** A federal judge had ruled that the company could not flood credit-reporting agencies with requests to place fraud alerts on LifeLock customers' credit files without information that its members were about to become victims of fraud.

- **LifeLock had agreed to pay $12 million to settle charges of unfair and deceptive trade practices.** The Federal Trade Commission (FTC) had investigated consumer complaints against LifeLock, and the company ultimately agreed to stop making claims that it: protects against all forms of identity theft; prevents unauthorized changes to members' mailing addresses; constantly monitors activity on members' consumer credit reports; and ensures that members receive a call from creditors before opening a new credit account in their names.

- **Former LifeLock employees had accused the company of misleading, unfair, and deceptive practices.** In two lawsuits, former LifeLock insiders claimed the company failed to notify members with fraud alerts; manipulated fraud alerts to its elderly customers; failed to staff its security team with experienced people; and neglected to protect its own members' information from potential data breaches.

Eleven months after Ebarle's class-action suit, LifeLock agreed to pay a record $100 million to consumers to settle the suit and the deceptive advertising charges by the FTC.[2] LifeLock would neither confirm nor deny the allegations, and claimed the FTC charges "related to advertisements that we no longer run and policies that are no longer in place." After the settlement announcement, Todd Davis, cofounder of LifeLock, resigned his position as CEO.[3] Davis had earlier gained attention for his brash 2006 marketing campaign that plastered his Social Security number in television, newspaper, and Internet ads, and claimed that LifeLock's protection of his Social

Security number made it "useless to a criminal." Davis suffered thirteen instances of identity theft following the campaign.[4]

The FTC's website offers this bit of advice to people considering purchasing identity theft protection: "Before you pay for a service, evaluate it and its track record before you pay any fees."[5]

Rule #18: Don't Waste Money on Identity Theft Protection Services

When we started the project that led to this book, we wanted to develop a personal cybersecurity program that would be effective, affordable, and easy to achieve. Hopefully, you'll take the actions we've recommended throughout *Hack-Proof Your Life Now!* But people being people, we want the easiest solution to cybersecurity, including us. So it's no surprise that friends, family members, and the public we meet at our trainings often ask us if they should subscribe to LifeLock or a similar service that promises protection against identity theft. We especially get this question after the headlines trumpet new data-breach stories and the follow-on advertising plugs identity protection services. Our answer to this natural question is an unequivocal, "No!"

We don't recommend using these services for three practical reasons:[6]

1. **Identity protection companies** *don't offer* **you the strongest protection—the Security Freeze.** Only you can close your unguarded credit files by putting them on Security Freeze, also known as a Credit Freeze, which we explained in chapter 10. No ID-theft service can do that for you. All three credit-reporting agencies require you, the consumer, to contact them to put a freeze on your file.

2. **Many identity protection firms promote an inherently unsafe approach called Credit Monitoring, which assumes**

you want your credit files opened. That means anyone can easily and quickly add credit to your name—either you or an impersonator. The ID-theft services will notify you if they detect new credit has been added to your files. Of course, if they do and you didn't authorize that new credit, then you have an identity theft problem. In essence, Credit Monitoring notifies you of trouble after the fact. That's not smart cybersecurity. Better to simply keep your credit files closed—frozen—and then lift the freeze the few times you need to add credit.

3. **You're the best person to protect your identity—at practically no cost compared to identity theft services.** When *Consumer Reports* covered LifeLock's $100 million settlement with the FTC, it made this observation: "If you're concerned about LifeLock or identity-protection services in general, remember that you can take important steps to protect your identity for little or no cost." (We've showed you those steps throughout this book.) LifeLock and its growing list of competitors want you to hire them to protect your identity and they offer consumers a dizzying array of multi-tier subscriptions: credit-report monitoring, black-market searches for your Social Security number, lost-wallet help, address-change alerts, credit-score tracking, password management, identity repair, and even $1 million identity-theft insurance. Those features sound impressive and will cost you about $100 to $300 a year, but you won't get the all-powerful Security Freeze at all three credit bureaus.[7] The Security Freeze is the Achilles' heel of the identity protection industry. Why would anyone want to pay up to $300 a year for a service that doesn't actually stop identity theft, especially when you can place a Security Freeze on your credit files for a one-time fee of $30 or less?

If ID-theft services really wanted to offer the safest protection *against* identity theft, they'd tell people to place their credit files on Security Freeze. But if everyone realized they could easily freeze and unfreeze their credit files, no valid business reason would exist for companies to monitor your closed credit files. Identity thieves couldn't penetrate the Security Freeze to take out fraudulent credit in your name. They'd be out of business. In essence, open credit files mean good business for banks, identity-protection companies, and identity thieves. Closed credit files mean good cybersecurity for you.

Your Total Cybersecurity Control

We don't recommend firms that promise ID-theft protection at this time because of the quality of the services. Our other chief reason for not recommending these programs is philosophical. The value proposition of the identity-theft-protection services doesn't align with being omniscient about your financial affairs. We firmly believe that *you* must be at the center of the important responsibility of maintaining strong security. Only from that all-knowing role over your financial life can you achieve total clarity and confidence in your security. You, and only you, must control your cybersecurity so you can enjoy a hack-proofed life.

Hack-Proof Action Step #18

Time to take action. This book is about closing your cybersecurity gap and boosting your safety. We want to motivate you right now to move from thinking about hack-proofing your life to actually making it happen. So just turn the page to see how we propose you add the New Cybersecurity Rules to your life.

19

Get It Done—Boost Your Cybersecurity Today

Take a Pledge
to Hack-Proof Your Life

We know from research that people will more likely complete an action if they write it down.[1] To get you started, we recommend you make a personal commitment to boost your cybersecurity. Please read the Hack-Proof Action Pledge below, pick three things you'll start immediately, give yourself a deadline for the rest, and sign your commitment. Then turn the page to the Hack-Proof Action Step Checklist.

Hack-Proof Action Pledge

I commit to hack-proofing my life and boosting my safety by taking the actions described in the New Cybersecurity Rules. I will act immediately on three items below and complete the remainder by this deadline: __/__/____.

1. _____
_____
_____

2. _____
_____
_____

3. _____
_____
_____

Signature: _____

Hack-Proof Checklist

In her best-selling book *The Life-Changing Magic of Tidying Up*, author Marie Kondo offers a system for cleaning up our cluttered and disorganized homes and workspaces. A key Kondo principle involves tidying up one category at a time (clothes, books, papers, etc.).[2]

When we look at measures you must take to hack-proof your life, we think taking action by category makes sense, so we've created a checklist to guide you through the process of adopting the New Cybersecurity Rules. We've organized your steps by three convenient groups: software/services, financial institutions, and behaviors. Most actions take just minutes to complete. Consult the Hack-Proof Action Guide for details and guidance.

SOFTWARE/SERVICES

Action Step #1

☐ Create a secret email address for your financial accounts and set it up with the strongest possible security settings (two-step login verification, strong password and username).

Action Step #4

☐ Download a password manager and put it on all your computers and devices. Pick a strong master password using the mnemonic or poetic approach.

Action Step #5

☐ Install a VPN program on your mobile devices and laptops for safe use of free Wi-Fi.

Action Step #6

☐ Change your router's default username and password—don't keep the factory settings.

☐ Select the WPA or WPA2 encryption setting.

☐ Disable the WPS setting on your router.

☐ Update your router's software.

Action Step #7

☐ Create passcodes for your smartphones and tablets.

☐ Activate the "Find My iPhone" or "Locate My Device" app, in case your device becomes lost or stolen.

☐ Add emergency contact information to your devices.

Action Step #8

☐ Review and strengthen your social media privacy settings.

☐ Reexamine your "friends" to ensure you're still comfortable sharing with them.

Action Step #13

☐ Install and update antivirus software on your computers and devices.

Action Step #15

☐ Back up your data on ALL your devices to at least two locations—the cloud and a physical device.

FINANCIAL INSTITUTIONS

Action Step #3

☐ Enable two-step verification on all your key accounts that allow it—financial accounts and personal email.

Action Step #9

☐ Create text or email alerts for your bank accounts and credit cards.

Action Step #10

☐ Place a Security Freeze on your credit files at all three reporting agencies: Equifax, Experian, and TransUnion.

Action Step #11

☐ Request a search on your children's Social Security numbers at all three credit bureaus.

☐ Review your state's laws to determine the best way to protect your children from identity theft.

BEHAVIOR

Action Step #2

☐ Create stronger passwords using mnemonic, goal-setting, or poetic password approaches.

Action Step #12

☐ Understand how to inspect any ATM or payment kiosk for possible skimming fraud.

☐ Avoid using non-bank ATMs for withdrawing cash.

Action Step #14

☐ Always update your programs when prompted and set them to update automatically, if that's an option.

☐ Uninstall or disable unsafe software programs and programs you don't use.

☐ Regularly update your smartphone and tablet software and apps.

Action Step #16

☐ Learn how to unmask an email's true sender on the display-name line.

☐ Understand how to examine an email message for the key signs of fraud.

Action Step #17

☐ Know how to inspect links in suspicious emails to determine if they're real or fraudulent.

☐ Recognize the danger of opening any unsolicited email attachment.

Hack-Proof
Action Guide

Welcome to Our Hack-Proof Action Guide

The following sections will offer you guidance, tips, and insights on implementing the Action Steps associated with the New Cybersecurity Rules. Many of our recommendations should be easy to achieve in a short period of time; others may take a bit longer and involve doing things with your computer or device that you've not previously done. Depending on your technical proficiency, in some cases you may want to seek the assistance of your favorite computer guru.

In order to have maximum hack-proof protection, you may need to acquire some new software or services, such as a password manager, antivirus software, or data-backup hardware and cloud storage. These often involve some small expense, though free options typically exist, too. We've researched these topics and the following pages will introduce you to well-reviewed products and services to consider when it comes to taking action. Of course, you can always find more by searching on Google. Regardless, it's important not to become paralyzed with too many choices or too much research. Taking action now needs to take precedent—you can always change, upgrade, or improve on your security choices later. But right now, you want to close your cybersecurity gaps quickly and boost your security by taking action. The following guide will help you.

Action Step #1:
Create a Secret Email Address

We're glad you're taking this action because it will boost your security by reducing the number of places hackers may find the email you use for your financial accounts. Before you proceed with setting up your financial-only address, though, it's important to familiarize yourself with the key issues we covered in chapter 2 and chapter 4 about strong passwords and two-step verification. You'll need to know these concepts so you can set up the best protection for your new account. If you haven't done so yet, read those chapters now.

When it comes to choosing a service, you probably know some of the big names: Gmail, Yahoo, AOL, Outlook (formerly Hotmail), and iCloud (formerly Me.com). As you make your choice and set up an account, follow these guidelines:

- **Email address**: Avoid using any personal information about yourself when you create your address—the portion that comes before the @ sign. Chapter 2 offers approaches to follow.

- **Password:** Naturally, for your secret email you'll want a very strong password. Again, chapter 2 can help you. Remember to include some numbers and symbols.

- **Two-step protection**: Set up your account so it has a two-step login process, which all good providers offer. See Action Step #3 for more details.

- **Password reset**: If offered, choose the safer telephone recovery option to reset your password. If not, make certain you pick a password reset question that's difficult to guess.

Take these actions as you set up your secret email address and you'll have stronger security.

Estimated Completion Time: Less than ten minutes

Action Step #2:
Beat the Password Paradox

Strong passwords frustrate hackers. And nearly everyone can make improvements to their passwords, as you've seen in chapter 2. One of the best ways to boost password strength involves adding numbers and symbols to your secret passcode. When you choose a password phrase—a lyric, poem, or goal—be sure to pick a few characters or words that can be turned into symbols. A phrase laced with symbols will strengthen any password. Use the conversion chart below for guidance on how to replace the following words or letters with symbols to make your password phrase stronger but still easy to remember.

Letter-to-Symbol Conversion	
Change this...	**To this...**
At	@
For	4
To, Too, Two	2
S	$
I	1 or !
E	3
A	4 or @
O	0
T	+
And	&
More	>
Less	<

The skills you learned in chapter 2 will also help you create the only password you really need to remember: the one that operates your password manager. See Hack-Proof Action Step #4 on page 141 for direction.

Estimated Completion Time: Less than two minutes

Action Step #3:
Choose Two-Step Verification

Adding two-step authentication to your email and financial accounts signals that you take your security seriously—a key step to hack-proofing your life. Before long this security approach, or a more advanced one, will become standard.

Financial Accounts

To boost your security, you'll want to set two-step verification for your online bank and credit accounts. Every bank's website differs, but you'll want to look under your profile or account settings. Find the security or privacy section and look for two-step verification. Note: Some banks may use terms other than two-step verification. For example, Chase calls its version Identification Code, while Bank of America uses SafePass.

If you can't find the two-step verification setting, don't worry but don't give up. Contact your bank's customer service by calling the number on its website. They will explain how to set up this important security feature.

Email Accounts

You also want to put two-step verification on your email accounts, including your primary and financial-only addresses. Here's some guidance on where to find the two-step settings at the top providers.

- **Gmail:** To set up two-step verification on your Gmail account visit: www.google.com/2step. While logged into your account, click the circle at the top of the page and then select My Account. Under Sign-in & Security choose Signing in to Google. Then turn on 2-Step Verification.

  Google gives you a couple of two-step options. You can choose to have a code sent via text message or get Google to call you and provide the code over the phone. You will need to enter the code before you can successfully access your account.

  Don't worry, you won't need to do this each time you log in. You can designate safe devices through Gmail and won't need to enter a code every time you want to use the account. When signing in on a personal (private) computer, check "Don't ask again on this computer."

  Another option is called Google Authenticator—an app you can download on your smartphone that will generate the secret code without any Internet connection. You will need to open the app when signing in to your account to access the code. Download the program from the app store you use.

  You also can use a physical security key, sometimes called a key fob. This device stays linked to your account and continuously generates new codes. To use a security key for Gmail, you will have to purchase the fob separately (about $30 to $50) and set it up on the site. Gmail will walk you through the setup.

- **Yahoo:** Once you successfully create your email address, click the gear icon and then Account Info. Sign in again. Next, click Account Security and then Two-step Verification. Yahoo will give you three options. You can have a code sent to your phone via text message or receive a phone call with the code. By default, you will only need to enter a code the first time you sign into your account from a new device.

If you have the Yahoo app on your phone, you can also use the Yahoo Account Key. To enable it, open the Yahoo app and tap your Profile image. You will see a key icon that represents Account Key—click on that. Click through to view a sample notification and see how the app works. Finish the setup by tapping Yes to enable the program.

Once you've enabled Account Key, you won't need to enter your password or a special code. When you sign in to your Yahoo account, a notification will be sent to your phone. You will tap Yes to verify that you're signing in to your account.

- **AOL:** AOL also offers free email with two-step verification. Once you have entered your information and created your email address, visit the Account page and sign in again. Under the 2-Factor Authentication section, select Setup. Next, enter your phone number and choose text message or phone call to receive your code. AOL will send you the verification, which you will enter. Then click Verify and select Turn On.

- **Outlook:** Anyone can create a free email account at Outlook .com, the same services as Microsoft's Live.com. Once you create your account, sign in. Choose the Security & Privacy option on the page header. Scroll down and select Set Up Two-Step Verification. You can verify your identity with a phone number, an alternate email address, or the Windows app. If you select a phone number, Microsoft will send you the code via text message. To generate login codes without an Internet connection, you can also download the Microsoft Authenticator or the Google Authenticator.

Estimated Completion Time: Less than two minutes

Action Step #4:
Get a Password Manager

A password manager will enhance your safety and make your online life easier. We initially resisted the idea but changed our minds after trying them and observing their safety, effectiveness, and ease of use. We recommend you take the plunge, because these services boost your security and eliminate the need to clog your brain remembering weak passwords.

Most password managers have paid and free versions of their software. Of course, they also offer two-step verification security. The free versions usually work only on one device; with a paid version, you can sync your password manager to your computer, smartphone, tablet, and any other device you use. Some options include:

- **Dashlane**: This widely used password manager has both a paid and free version. The paid version, Dashlane Premium, costs $39.99 per year and covers all your devices. The free version only works on one device. Both Premium and Free store your encrypted passwords on your device (locally). The two versions also generate strong passwords, use autofill technology to complete forms with your information, rate your current passwords, and have two-step verification. In addition, Dashlane Premium also allows you to back up your encrypted password file to the cloud, send encrypted versions of your passwords to others, and access your passwords from the Internet on any device.

- **LastPass**: Like Dashlane, LastPass offers a free and paid version. LastPass Premium costs $12 per year and can be used on an unlimited number of devices. LastPass differs from Dashlane because it stores your encrypted passwords in the cloud rather than on your local device. The premium and free versions will automatically fill in forms and alert you to weak passwords. Both versions offer two-step verification as well as "One Time Passwords." LastPass Premium also has an option for sharing password folders with family members or others.

- **1Password**: This password manager has two service tiers: 1Password and 1Password Families. A single user can get 1Password for a one-time purchase of $64.99. 1Password Families costs $5 per month for up to five people and additional members cost $1 extra per month. Each family member will have his or her own account, but you can easily share information with others via the app. Both the single and family programs allow you to install the program on all of your devices and have autofill technology and a password generator.

- **iCloud Keychain**: Apple's password manager, iCloud Keychain, is available on iPhones and iPads running iOS 7.0.3 or higher and Macs running OS X Mavericks v10.9 or above. You can enable iCloud Keychain on your phone or tablet through the Security settings. Tap iCloud and then toggle iCloud Keychain on. If you are using a Mac, go to System Preferences in the Apple menu and choose iCloud. Then click Keychain and follow the instructions. The service is free. Keychain will store your passwords with strong encryption. You'll have to create a master password called iCloud Security Passcode. Note: Not all sites are compatible with iCloud Keychain yet.

- **KeePass:** This password manager will appeal to the sophisticated computer user. KeePass is a free, open-source program that you can download and use on all of your devices. It involves a lot of intimidating settings you don't encounter with the more automated password managers. Your passwords are stored locally and you can download browser plugins so KeePass will autofill your logins. It also has tough two-step verification options and can help you generate unique passwords.

Take the Time

You can get started with a password manager quickly. Once you've set up your account, you'll start adding new passwords into the manager as you visit different sites—ones you frequent and new ones, too. Be sure to spend half an hour at the outset to familiarize yourself with the way your manager works and how it appears on your computer and devices. That will promote a smoother transition to this new level of high security.

Estimated Completion Time: Less than thirty minutes

Action Step #5:
Use Free Public Wi-Fi Cautiously

While it's okay to use free Wi-Fi—except for checking your email or conducting financial transactions—if you need to use public Wi-Fi often, you should have a Virtual Private Network (VPN). This program will encrypt your activities, preventing thieves from watching and recording what you do. There are many options. Some free VPNs will give you basic security but are usually supported by advertisements.[1] You can also purchase a subscription to a virtual network service, which will vary in price from $2 to $10 per month. Remember, we're not just talking about your laptop—you'll also want to use a VPN app for your smartphone and tablet if you use free Wi-Fi often.

Paid VPN Services

The following VPN services run on all popular operating systems for computers and devices. Typically, a subscription includes up to five devices. Free versions often include advertisements. To learn more about the programs, just search on Google by service name.

- **NordVPN:** $48 per year.

- **Private Internet Access:** $39.95 per year.

- **Spotflux Premium:** $37.99 per year or $29.99 for one device.

- **HotSpot Shield Elite:** $29.95 and a free version.

- **CyberGhost**: Free with advertisements.

- **VPNBook**: Free, open-source program. No advertisements but can be difficult to use.

Estimated Completion Time: Less than five minutes

Action Step #6:
Secure Your Home Wi-Fi Network

Securing your home wireless system sounds more challenging than actually doing it. Just follow our directions below to improve your wireless network safety. If you get confused, consult your Wi-Fi router's user manual, a good resource easily found on the Internet. Or you might want assistance from your tech guru or a family member who knows computers. (A new generation of routers will make this very easy in the future. But if you need help, get it.)

Before we get started, you need to gather some information about your router:

Your router's name: To begin, find the name of your router's manufacturer and write it down. Look on the underside of the router. In many cases, it will identify the brand of the router. Some examples: Cisco Linksys, Linksys XAC1900, Belkin AC1200DB, and Netgear Nighthawk.

Router's model number: Look in the same area for your router's model number, which is often right under the maker's name. The model number will be followed by a combination of numbers and letters such as WRT110, F5D8236-4. You can see the arrow pointing to the model number below. Write down the model number.

Source: Netgear

Your router's IP address: Identifying your router's IP address takes just a second. IP stands for Internet Protocol, a numeric label assigned to each device connected to a network. Your router either has its original IP address or a new one from when you set it up at home. If you don't know your router's IP address, follow these instructions.[2]

- **Windows computer:** Click the Start button and type Command Prompt into the search bar. A black box will pop up. Now type ipconfig/all and hit Enter. Scroll down and find Default Gateway. Your IP address is the series of numbers you see there and will look something like this: 192.168.1.1 Write down your numbers.

- **Apple computer:** Click the Apple icon and choose System Preferences. Next click Network. If you are connected via Wi-Fi, select Wi-Fi Connection. However, when using an Ethernet connection, choose Wired Ethernet Connection. Then click Advanced. On the header, choose TCP/IP, and the series of numbers next to Router is your IP address.

Some router manufacturers, including Netgear, use an app you can download on your computer, smartphone, or tablet to control your router settings. For these routers, download the app on your device and open that to configure your router settings. From the app, you can change your router username, password, and encryption settings, and update your firmware. If your router uses an app, you won't need to find your router's IP address.

Note: If you have never changed your router's IP address and don't know it, go to the manufacturer's website (Linksys, Netgear, Belkin, etc.). Next, go to the company's support page and search for your router using the router make or model number. Download the user manual and scroll through until you find the IP address. Write it down. It will look something like this:

How to open the browser-based utility

To access some advanced settings, you need to open the browser-based utility.

To open the browser-based utility:

1. Run Linksys Connect, click **Change** under *Router settings*, click **Advanced settings**, then click **OK**.

   – or –

   Open a web browser on a computer connected to your network, then go to **192.168.1.1**.

   The router prompts you for a user name and password.

Source: Linksys

Step One: Change Username and Password

Now that you've collected the router information, start securing your network. First, you must create a new username and password. Open a web browser and type in your router's IP address. You will be prompted to log in with your wireless router's current username and password, the same credentials you use to connect to its wireless signal.

Once you log in, find the Security or Administrative tab. Enter a new username and password in the appropriate fields. Make sure you change both. Don't keep the default username and password that came with your router as cyber criminals could easily guess them. After you've created a unique username and password, click Save and Apply.[3]

Step Two: Encrypt

Next, find the Wireless Security or Wireless Network. Those settings should enable you to change the wireless encryption type to the most secure option. Choose WPA2, WPA2-PSK, or WPA2-ENT. The last one, designed for businesses, is the most secure router encryption setting today.[4] Restart your router and reconnect all of your devices. But you're not done yet.

Step Three: Disable WPS

The WPS feature allows you to quickly connect your devices to your home network without needing to enter your Wi-Fi password. If you don't disable it, you will have a huge security hole.

To disable WPS, log in to your router again, just like above, and look for Wi-Fi Protected Setup or WPS in the interface. From there, see your options for disabling WPS. If you can, you should disable WPS altogether. However, some routers won't let you. At the very least, you should disable the PIN or put a limit on the number of guesses someone can take before gaining access. Both of these options will help, but you may want to purchase a router that allows you to disable the feature completely.[5] Newer routers have better security and can be easier to use.

Step Four: Update Your Router's Firmware

Most consumer wireless routers arrive already running outdated and unsecure firmware (a fancy word for the software installed on your router). You need to update that software to keep your wireless network secure. Updating the firmware reminds us of replacing a fuse on your home's breaker panel—it sounds bad, but once you get started, it's a simple fix.

The instructions below will walk you through the process.[6] Check your router's user manual if you face any difficulty. Remember, just take it one step at a time.

Things You Need Before Starting

- Your router
- A laptop or computer
- An Ethernet cable

How to Discover What Firmware Your Router Is Running

Type your router's IP address into your browser, then log in using your router's username and password. On this page, called your router's Default Gateway, you can see the firmware version that your router currently runs. To spot the number, look to the top right-hand corner or below the Host Name and Domain Name on the main page.

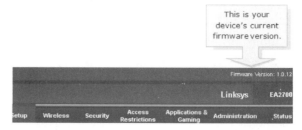

Source: Linksys

But What Version Should You Be Running?

You've completed the hard part. Now you just need to determine if you have outdated firmware on your router. Go back to the manufacturer's website and search on the router model number again to find the router's Downloads page. It may be under Product Details, Software, or Downloads. Click Downloads to see the newest version. If it doesn't match the firmware currently on your router, you will need to download it. Click Download and then Save. Put the firmware download somewhere on your computer that you can find it, such as your desktop or downloads folder.

Update Your Firmware

Time to update your router's firmware. Note: You will need your Ethernet cable to connect the router to your computer. Connect via Ethernet cable when updating firmware, as it's a more secure approach than doing so wirelessly. If you don't have an Ethernet cable, you can use the one already connected to your router. Simply plug the other end (the one that's is currently plugged into your wall) into your laptop or computer.

Go back to your router's Default Gateway landing page (the one you found by entering the IP address) and click on the Security or Administration tab (depending on your router). Find Firmware Upgrade. There you can browse for the software you saved to your desktop. When you find it, click Open and then Start Upgrade. When your router completes the update, it will reboot. Check your router's Default Gateway page to confirm the new firmware version loaded.

You're All Done

Congratulations! You've successfully updated your firmware and closed your network off from hackers. Most router manufacturers don't send out update notifications for a new version of firmware, so every so often you'll want to check and make sure you have the newest version.

Estimated Completion Time: Less than sixty minutes

Action Step #7:
Add Passcodes to Your Devices

In the early days of smartphones, a four-digit passcode secured your phone. Now, both Apple and Android have boosted their security options. New iPhones running iOS 9 or higher have six-digit passcodes by default, two digits more than original passcode programs. The six-digit passcode increases the possible combination from ten thousand to one million—offering greater hacking protection.[7] You can move to a six-digit PIN on older iPhones running iOS 9 through the Touch ID & Passcode section in Settings. Just begin the Change Passcode process and then tap Passcode Options to see your choices.

Android phones offer a lock pattern, four-digit passcode, or up to a sixteen-character password. The lock pattern allows you to draw a pattern on a grid of dots. Security experts warn that others could guess your pattern by seeing fingerprints on the phone.[8] The sixteen-character password provides the most security. You can choose from these options in your Settings.

Locate My Phone Apps

To combat the soaring number of smartphone thefts, Apple, Google, and Samsung added a kill-switch feature. It allows you to remotely turn off and lock your phone or tablet, and even delete the data on a lost or stolen device.[9]

Apple's Find My iPhone will lock your screen and display a message with your alternate phone number, allowing the finder to call you. Find My iPhone tracks the location of a stolen iPhone or iPad on a map by signing in to your iCloud account from another device or computer.

If you use a newer iPhone or an iPad running iOS 7 or higher, you can activate Apple's Find My iPhone through iCloud. Go to Settings, then iCloud and sign in with your Apple ID. Scroll down and toggle on Find My iPhone.

You will also see the option to Send Last Location, which sends its location to Apple anytime its battery gets critically low. If your phone dies when missing, you will be able to see its last location on a map through iCloud.

Also, give Find My iPhone location permissions. From the Settings menu, click Privacy and then Location Services. Toggle on the button next to Find My iPhone.

When you start the Find My iPhone process, another feature, Activation Lock, automatically begins working. Activation Lock foils a thief's effort to sell your phone on the black market because they will need your Apple ID and password to turn off the phone, erase it, or deactivate it.

Find My iPhone also allows you to remotely erase the data on your device in extra-sensitive personal or business situations. Older Apple devices running iOS 6 have limited Find My iPhone features. You should update your device for the best protection.

Google released a comparable feature called Android Device Manager. To activate it, connect your device to your Google account. Find the Google Settings on your phone (usually under Settings), and then click Security. Go to Android Device Manager and make sure that Remotely Locate This Device and Allow Remote Lock and Factory Reset are turned on. Next, turn on Location Access to track your phone remotely. To do that, you just go to Settings and tap Location.

Remember, these security features change and improve all the time. Our hack-proof advice: become familiar with how these features work and use them to the fullest.

Identifying Your Phone

Quickly report lost or stolen phones to the police and your mobile carrier. You'll need to identify the device to prove ownership, so be sure you have the phone's serial, model, and unique identification numbers.[10] You can find them in your phone's settings. For Apple devices, go to Settings, General, and About. On Android phones, visit Settings, About, and then Status. You can also find your Apple or Android device's unique identification number by dialing *#06#. Record these numbers and keep them in a safe, accessible place like Dropbox or Evernote.

Two final precautions: be alert when using your phone in public because phone thieves target distracted victims. And, of course, never leave your phone unattended.

What About Emergencies?

New iPhones come pre-installed with the Health app, which you can't delete. This app includes a Medical ID section to store your emergency contacts and other important details. To activate it, open the Health app and choose Medical ID on the bottom row. Click Edit and select Show When Locked so your emergency contact information can be found even from your locked screen.

To view a Medical ID on a locked phone, tap the Emergency button when you swipe to unlock a phone. On the next screen, tap

Medical ID. Android phones have similar features. Go to Settings and then Security. On the Owner Info section, complete the In Case of Emergency (ICE) fields. Now you can lock your phone and know that someone could access your emergency contacts when needed.

In Case of Emergency Apps

If your phone does not come with a pre-installed ICE option, you still want to ensure an emergency responder or a Good Samaritan can reach your emergency contact. Use your note-taking app for the easiest approach. Type your emergency contact information and any health information you want to share in the note, then take a screenshot and set that image as your lock-screen wallpaper.

Some highly rated ICE contact apps for iPhone and Android include:

- ICE Standard ER with Smart911™– Cost: $0.99 App Store/ Free Google Play

- ICE: In Case of Emergency – Cost: $3.99[11]

Estimated Completion Time: Less than five minutes

Action Step #8:
Tighten Your Privacy Settings on Social Media

The fun in social media involves sharing news and photos with your friends and family. Unfortunately, hackers have taken advantage of people's loose security settings to obtain their personal information to use in hacks and other frauds. Good cybersecurity requires having strong privacy settings. Take a moment now to review your privacy settings on all your social media profiles, including these:

- **Facebook:** Click the triangle next to Account at the top-right corner of your Facebook page. From there, select Settings and then Privacy. You can choose different settings questions such as, Who can see my stuff? Facebook will provide you with options such as Only Me, Friends Only, and Public. Then you can select the option that best fits your privacy needs.

Selecting Only Me will keep your posts totally private—meaning no one but you can see them. Choosing Friends Only means that only your Facebook friends can see the post. Public means your profile can be viewed by anyone who searches your name, whether a Facebook friend or not.

You can also create custom lists such as Family or Close Friends and only share items with those lists. And you can change your privacy settings post by post: For each post you make, you'll see a drop-down box from which you can select your audience for the specific post. The main options include Public (anyone searching for you) or Friends. You can also select More Options to customize who sees the post. In addition, you can choose who sees posts that others make on your timeline.

Facebook has another feature called Privacy Checkup, which can also be found in the drop-down box on the upper-right corner of your Facebook page. The Privacy Checkup allows you to check and edit your basic privacy settings in one place. You can also review how your Facebook profile looks to other people by going to your privacy settings.

- **Twitter:** The default Public setting means anyone can see your tweets and follow you without your approval. However, by setting your Twitter account to Protected, only those you've approved as followers can view your tweets. Go to the Security and Privacy Settings section on your Twitter feed. Find the Tweet Privacy section and check the box next to Protect My Tweets. Make sure you click the Save button at the bottom of the page. You will need to enter your password to save the change.

- **Instagram:** Instagram's default Public setting allows anyone to view your photos and follow you. However, you can change your account to Private, which allows only your approved followers to see your Instagram posts. You must use the Instagram app to change your account to Private. First, visit your profile on the app and then find the Settings button. From there you can turn on Private Account. By switching your account to Private, you can also control who can follow you. Anyone wishing to follow your account will have to send you a request, which you can approve or ignore.

- **LinkedIn:** This is a different situation than other social media accounts, as you want others to have access to your LinkedIn information. However, you still need to protect yourself and your account. Your profile's summary can be viewed by anyone on LinkedIn, so don't share your email address, phone number, or home address. You should also only connect with people you know and trust, or who share a trusted, mutual connection.

Two-Step Verification for Social Media

We're going to say it again: You really need two-step verification for all of your online accounts, and that means your social media accounts, too. Facebook created its own version of two-step verification called Login Approvals. This program requires you to enter a code sent to your mobile device when logging in to your Facebook account from an unrecognized device. You can opt into Login Approvals by choosing Account Security in your Account Settings page.

Twitter has Login Verification, which sends a six-digit code to your mobile number on file when logging in to your account. Go to the Account Settings page of your Twitter account and select Verify Login Requests. You'll be prompted to enter your phone number and a confirmed email address.

Instagram was slow to join the two-step verification game, but it now has the technology. Like Facebook and Twitter, the popular photo-sharing app will send a code to your phone when you log in. To set this up, first update your Instagram app to the latest version, then go to the Settings page and click Two-Factor Authentication.

Be sure to set up two-step verification on your LinkedIn account, as well. A hacker could post embarrassing things for your professional contacts to see if they gain access your account. Log in to your account and then hover your mouse over your picture in the right-hand corner. Choose Manage next to Privacy and Settings. Next click on Account on the side of the page and then Manage Security Settings. Then you can turn two-step verification on. You'll be prompted to enter the code sent to your mobile device anytime you log in from a new computer.

Estimated Completion Time: Less than ten minutes

Action Step #9:
Put Alerts on Your Bank and Credit Cards

Getting notifications for your credit card and debit card transactions will boost your security quickly. Any strange charges or outflows of money will come to your attention right away. Each financial institution sets up its alert system differently and you should log in to your account or contact your card issuer for specific instructions.

For many cards, you will need to customize the "track your spending" feature. In this setting, you can set alerts for any purchases over a certain dollar amount. Set that amount to the minimum ($1 or lower) so you get an alert for all charges. In many cases, thieves will test the card with small purchases first, so catching these can help prevent larger fraud.

While you are changing these settings, you should also activate the "fraud alerts" feature on your card. With this alert, your bank or credit card company will contact you if they notice any unusual activity on your account. Of course, your spending alerts should notify you of anything strange, but it doesn't hurt to have the extra security.[12]

Estimated Completion Time: Less than ten minutes

Action Step #10:
Freeze Your Credit Files

Putting a Security Freeze on your credit files establishes a solid defense against identity theft. Doing so takes only a few minutes online or over the phone. Each of the three bureaus handles the process slightly differently.

- **Online:** Experian and TransUnion ask a few questions to verify your identity. (What's your mortgage or loan payment? What's your street address?) Both allow you to create your PIN for controlling your file and email you a confirmation that you completed the Security Freeze. TransUnion requires you to create an account before starting. Equifax doesn't ask verification questions, assigns you a PIN, and gives you a PDF to print and save for your records.

- **Telephone:** The process is similar on the phone. Equifax and TransUnion involve speaking to a live agent. Experian lets you complete the process answering prompts through your phone. All three will send confirmations by mail. Each takes less than five minutes.

- **Fees:** Credit file regulations vary by state and so do the fees associated with placing or lifting a Security Freeze. If you have a verified identity theft report, the bureaus typically waive your fees. Otherwise, your charges will range from free to $10.

Note: Keep in mind that it may take a few days for the freeze to be lifted after your request, so be sure to request a lift a few days before you need to access your credit. Also, you may need to temporarily lift your freeze when setting up your "my Social Security account" at the Social Security website.

Equifax	**Experian**	**TransUnion**
Equifax, Inc.	Experian, Inc.	TransUnion LLC
P.O. Box 740241	P.O. Box 4500	P.O. Box 2000
Atlanta, GA	Allen, TX	Chester, PA
30374	75013	19022-2000
866-349-5191	888-397-3742	888-909-8872
www.equifax.com	www.experian.com	www.transunion.com

Check Your Credit Report

As you take total control over your security, don't overlook checking your credit file. Twenty-five percent of U.S. adults have never checked their credit file for fraudulent charges or accounts. The law entitles you to one free credit report from each of the credit bureaus each year—go over it carefully to maintain good security.[13]

Canada

Unfortunately, Canadian residents cannot place a Security Freeze on their credit files. Currently Canada only offers a Credit File Alert (sometimes called Potential Fraud Alerts) for consumers. With this alert in place, creditors must contact you and verify your identity before granting credit. Since Canadians cannot get a Security Freeze, each year they should request and review free copies of their credit reports from both bureaus, Equifax Canada and TransUnion Canada.[14]

How to Set Up a Credit File Alert

You will need to request a Credit File Alert with both national credit bureaus in Canada.

Equifax Canada

To add this extra layer of protection to your Equifax credit file, call customer service at 800-465-7166.

TransUnion Canada

TransUnion Canada has a Potential Fraud Alert form online for you to fill out. You can find this form on their website (www.transunion .ca). Under the Identity Theft heading on the bottom, click where you see "Help avoid fraud by requesting that creditors contact you before deciding to extend your credit."

Print out the form and send it to the address provided. You will also need to include a copy of your photo ID and another form of identification such as a utility bill, credit card statement, or Social Insurance card. A list of accepted documents is at the end of the form. You can also contact TransUnion's customer service at 800-663-9980, ext. 3.

Equifax Canada	TransUnion Canada
Box 190 Jean Talon Station	P.O. Box 338, LCD1
Montreal, Quebec H1S 2Z2	Hamilton, ON L8L 7W2
800-465-7166	800-663-9980, ext. 3
www.consumer.equifax.ca	www.transunion.ca

Estimated Completion Time: Less than fifteen minutes

Action Step #11:
Protect Your Child's Identity

Every parent with minor children needs to contact the three credit bureaus with the required documentation. Laws and regulations governing this issue differ by state. Use the checklist and sample letter below to get started.[15]

Child Identity-Theft Checklist:

☐ Letter to all three of the credit bureaus
☐ Copy of government-issued ID
☐ Proof of address
☐ Copy of child's Social Security number
☐ Copy of child's birth certificate

Sample Letter
Your Name
Street Address
City, State, Zip Code

Date:

To Whom It May Concern:

I am concerned that my child's information may have been used fraudulently. I am requesting a manual search of my child's file using their Social Security number. If a record is found, I am requesting a copy of the file. In addition, a security alert should be placed on my child's file and Social Security number.

Parent/Guardian Contact Information

First name:_____Last name: _____
Address:_____
City:_____   State: _____
Zip Code:_____
Phone number:_____

Child's Information

First name:_____Last name: _____
Address:_____
City:_____   State: _____
Zip Code:_____
Social Security Number:_____
Date of Birth: _____

Please find attached the following documentation for my request:

- A copy of my government-issued ID

- Proof of my address

- A copy of my child's Social Security number

- A copy of my child's birth certificate

Sincerely,

[Your Signature]

Mailing addresses for three credit reporting agencies:
Once you have customized the letter, send it to each of the credit bureaus below. Note: For TransUnion you must start the process online at the link provided.

Equifax	Experian	TransUnion: Must fill out a
Information	P.O. Box 9554	form online. If the company
Services LLC	Allen, TX	does find a file in your
Minor Child	75013	child's name, it will alert
P.O. Box 105139		you and give you further
Atlanta, GA		instructions. (https://www.
30348-5139		transunion.com/cred-
		it-disputes/child-identi-
		ty-theft-inquiry-form)

A Security Freeze for Your Children

The states listed below give parents or guardians the power to protect minor children with a Security Freeze. Some states have pending legislation, so if your state is not listed below, search Google to see if that remains true. Here are the states (July 2016) that allow you to create a credit report for your child and then freeze it:

Arizona	Louisiana	Ohio
Connecticut	Maine	Oregon
Delaware	Maryland	South Carolina
Florida	Michigan	Tennessee
Georgia	Montana	Texas
Illinois	Nebraska	Utah
Indiana	New York	Virginia
Iowa	North Carolina	Wisconsin

If you live in one of these states, you should contact each of the credit bureaus and request a Security Freeze for your child.[16]

- **Equifax:** 866-349-5191

- **Experian:** 888-397-3742

- **TransUnion:** You can begin the Security Freeze process online at https://www.transunion.com/credit-disputes/child-identity-theft-inquiry-form.

What to Do if Your State Does Not Protect Children

If your state law does not currently allow you to create a credit report for your child and freeze it, you should still act. Equifax allows any parent, regardless of state law, to open a credit file for a minor child and then freeze it—a good start. However, your child remains vulnerable, because no such feature exists at the other two credit bureaus.

Next, be sure to check for a credit report in your child's name once a year. Use the sample letter template to inquire about your child's record at the bureaus. This will allow you to catch any fraud early.

Finally, appeal to your elected officials. Contact your state representatives and ask them to introduce child identity-theft protection legislation similar to other states. (Who could oppose sensible legislation?) Your representatives in Washington also have an opportunity to act. The Protect Children from Identity Theft Act, introduced in the U.S. Congress in 2015, would allow parents to open and freeze a credit report for their child in all 50 states. It currently only has a 2 percent chance of being enacted.[17] Writing to your state and federal representatives and stating your concern about child identity theft can make a difference.

Canadian Residents

If you live in Canada, you must also check your child's credit status with the two credit bureaus. Use the sample letter below to write to Equifax Canada and TransUnion Canada.

Child Identity-Theft Checklist:
- ☐ Letter to both of the credit bureaus (Equifax and TransUnion)
- ☐ Copy of government-issued ID
- ☐ Proof of address
- ☐ Copy of child's SIN
- ☐ Copy of child's birth certificate

Sample Letter

Your Name
Street Address
Municipality, Province, Postal Code:

Date:

To whom it may concern:

I am concerned that my child's information may have been used fraudulently. I am requesting a manual search of my child's file using their Social Insurance number. If a record is found, I am requesting a copy of the file. In addition, a security alert should be placed on my child's file and Social Insurance number.

Parent/Guardian Contact Information:

First name:_____Last name: _____
Civic Address:_____
Municipality:_____　　Province: _____
Postal Code:_____　　Phone number:_____

Child's Information:

First name:_____Last name: _____
Civic Address:_____
Municipality:_____　　Province: _____
Postal Code:_____

Social Insurance Number:_____

Date of Birth: _____

Please find attached the following documentation for my request:

- A copy of my government-issued ID

- Proof of my address

- A copy of my child's Social Insurance number

- A copy of my child's birth certificate

Sincerely,

[Your Signature]

Equifax Canada Co.   **TransUnion Canada**

Box 190 Jean Talon Station   P.O. Box 338, LCD1

Montreal, Quebec H1S 2Z2   Hamilton, ON L8L 7W2

If a credit file exists, you should request a Potential Fraud Alert on the file. You can do so following the Canadian instructions above for Hack-Proof Action Step #10.

If a credit file does not exist, you should send this sample letter every year to check on your child's record. You should also protect your child's SIN.

Estimated Completion Time: About an hour

Action Step #12:
Watch for Skimming Devices

Unfortunately, sophisticated skimmer devices can be difficult to spot. You won't immediately notice that you've been scammed—another reason to set up text or email alerts on your payment cards. Seeing notices of money leaving your accounts or charged to your card puts you in the best position to catch skimming fraud. If you've not yet set up your alerts, see Hack-Proof Action Step #9.

Liability

The sooner you spot and report a card fraud, the better. Your liability in fraud cases increases the longer you wait to report a fraudulent charge. The table below shows how your liability increases with time.

Card Liability and Reporting Times	
When you report:	**Liability:**
Credit Card	
Any fraudulent charge at any time	$50
Debit Card	
Within two business days	$50
After two business days but before sixty calendar days after your statement	$500
More than sixty calendar days after your statement	Everything

Source: FTC

Note: You face NO liability for ANY fraudulent debit card transaction if your physical card was not lost or stolen and you report the fraud within sixty days of receiving your statement.

Estimated Completion Time: Less than one minute

Action Step #13:
Install Antivirus Software Now

In order to safely operate your computer, you must have working knowledge of your antivirus software. If you don't, as we've seen, you could easily tumble into a scam that takes advantage of your unfamiliarity with this aspect of computing behavior.

Most Windows computers come with the antivirus Microsoft Security Essentials program installed. You can open the program through the Start menu and then click Full Scan and the program will begin searching for malware and viruses.

Apple computers do not come with antivirus software installed. For years, a key selling point for Apple has been that its computers have stronger security and don't suffer from the plague of virus attacks we see in the Windows world. However, useful antivirus software designed for Macs warrants your attention and inclusion, as hackers do find ways to infiltrate Apple computers.

Choosing an Antivirus Software

If you don't have an antivirus program, please get one today. Many well-rated programs will provide you with solid protection. We've collected a list below of some popular, highly ranked, and well-known programs cited by computing magazines and software guides.

As a general rule, nearly all offer Mac, Windows, and Android versions as yearly subscriptions. The programs typically run in the background and give you the ability to manually scan and also schedule scans at different intervals. Some paid versions offer additional features such as ransomware protection, phishing protection, firewall (a network filter), and a password manager. Some offer free versions of their paid programs but will include advertisements; others are simply free but often not as robust as paid programs.

If you don't know which antivirus program you run or how it operates, hackers can prey on that uncertainty and trick you into falling for a phishing scam. Get protection and spend a little time learning your antivirus software. It will naturally boost your security.[18]

- **AVG AntiVirus Protection Pro:** $59.99 per year and works on an unlimited number of devices; operates on Windows, Mac, and Android devices. Free version pushes upgrade advertisements.

- **Avast Free Antivirus:** Runs on Windows, Mac, and Android. You must download a toolbar. Program pushes advertisements.

- **Bitdefender Antivirus Plus:** $39.95 for the year for one computer or $59.95 a year for three.

- **Kaspersky Antivirus:** $39.95 for one computer for one year or $59.95 for three computers.

- **McAfee Antivirus Plus**: $59.95 for the year, but you can use it on all of your devices—Windows, Mac, Android, and iOS.

- **Panda Free Antivirus:** Free. Windows only. Requires installing a toolbar on your browser.

- **Symantec Norton Security Deluxe**: $69.99 for the year to protect five devices. It works on Windows, Mac, Android, and iOS devices.

- **Webroot SecureAnywhere:** $39.99 for the year and covers one computer. You must be connected to the Internet to use the software.

Additional Malware Prevention

In addition to your antivirus protection, we recommend you add a free malware removal program called Malwarebytes that works on Windows and Mac. Your antivirus software does a great job with traditional viruses and some malware, but Malwarebytes excels at finding and removing damaging software that might get on your machine even if you have a good antivirus program. If your machine ever starts acting strangely, simply launch the Malwarebytes program and click Scan. Follow instructions from there.

You should run full scans on a regular basis to keep your system safe, because the program does not offer real-time protection like other antivirus software. But if malware is somehow found, Malwarebytes can remove the malware more effectively than most antivirus software. Malwarebytes can be used in your computer's Safe Mode, which helps if you've downloaded a nasty bug. Safe Mode allows your computer to run with just the basic operating system and stops additional programs from running.

Note: Businesses and commercial users must purchase Malwarebytes Premium for about $25. The free version will not protect a commercial network.[19]

Antivirus for Your Phone

Don't forget that your smartphones and tablets need good antivirus protection, too. The hackers definitely target them, and security experts anticipate more trouble on our devices in the future.

iPhone users: In 2015, Apple started pulling antivirus apps from its app store. The company believes that iOS works securely on its own.[20] If you search the iPhone app store for antivirus apps now, you will see some programs by big names. None of these apps offer true antivirus protection, though: rather, they do things like put an extra lock on your phone, include a "Find My iPhone" feature, and check whether your email has been compromised. They don't scan for viruses or warn you of a malicious link. In the case of Apple smartphones and tablets, just promptly update iOS when notified and you'll stay protected.

Android: Android phones do need antivirus apps—attacks on these devices continue to grow. Most apps cost about $10 to $30 a year. (There are some free ones, but do your research.) Some of the highest-rated antivirus apps for Android devices are Avast, Bitdefender, Kaspersky, and McAfee. Keep in mind that you may be able to apply your computer antivirus program to your phone as well.[21]

Estimated Completion Time: Less than thirty minutes

Control Downloads on Shared Computers

Your shared family computer can pose a cybersecurity threat depending on who uses it. However, you can control what other users download, which is probably your greatest potential problem. Just set yourself up as administrator of the computer: Only administrator accounts can download files, so make sure everyone else has a standard account and don't share the administrator password. Standard users will need you (the administrator) to enter the password anytime they need to download something.

On a Windows PC, first set up an administrator account. To do this, go to Settings (through the Start Menu) and select Accounts if you are using Windows 10. For earlier versions of Windows, go to Start and then Control Panel. An administrative account grants you the power to change security settings and install software. Don't use the administrator account as your day-to-day account—limit it to these security purposes.

Mac computers also have administrator accounts. When you first set up your computer, you probably created an administrator account, but to create a new one, go to System Preferences and then Accounts. Then click the + to add a new account and set as administrator. Just like on a Windows computer, only administrators can download files and make changes to the computer.[22]

Parental Controls

You can also set up parental controls. These limit the amount of time your kids spend on the computer, as well as what sites they can visit and what games they can play. On a Windows computer, set up these controls by going to the Control Panel and then User Accounts and Family Safety. For a Mac, go to System Preferences and click on Parental Controls. You can select each user and customize controls such as what apps and websites they can access, when and how long they can use the computer, whether or not they can use the webcam, and other activities.

Action Step #14:
Always Update Your Software
and Uninstall Unsafe Programs

Over time, people tend to accumulate software programs on their computers and devices that they've stopped using or updating. If this describes you, it's best to uninstall or disable them because they definitely represent security risks.

Additionally, some programs no longer receive support and updates, and therefore pose trouble. See below for our guidance on handling these problematic software programs.

QuickTime

As of 2016, Microsoft Windows users should stop running Apple QuickTime on their machine. The video-playing program no longer receives Windows security patches. In April, the Department of Homeland Security's U.S. Computer Emergency Readiness Team issued an alert to Windows users to uninstall QuickTime after discovering two serious security holes.[23] Since Apple no longer supports the software, the unsecured program leaves your machine open to attack.

If you still have QuickTime on your Windows device, uninstall it now. To uninstall, go to Start and open the Control Panel. Click Programs and Features and scroll down to QuickTime. Click once on the program name and then click Uninstall on the top bar.

The program remains safe for Mac users.

The PDF Reader, Flash, and Java Challenges

Many of us use two Adobe products that need special attention—Acrobat Reader and Flash Player. You can set your widely used PDF reader to automatically update in several ways.

To see your options, open your version of Acrobat Reader on your device. Click Edit then Preferences. Scroll down to Updater, where you will see four options. If you choose the first, Automatically Install Updates, Reader will install and update the new version of the program.

The second option automatically downloads updates but will not install them until you restart your computer. This may be a good option if you are concerned about your computer restarting at inopportune times.

The third option allows you to have Adobe notify you of an update, but you choose when to download and install. We don't recommend the fourth option, which essentially opts you out of being notified about automatic updates.

Choose the first or second options to stay hack-proofed, as they let you stay one step ahead. If you have trouble updating your preferences, you can also Google "Set automatic updates for Adobe Reader."

Flash Player, which makes websites interactive and delivers video and animations, poses a greater problem. Because Flash contains so many bugs, we recommend you uninstall the program and disable it in your web browsers.

Uninstall Adobe Flash

If you are on a Windows PC:

1. Download the Adobe Flash Player uninstaller from the Adobe website. (Visit https://helpx.adobe.com and search Adobe Flash and choose the Uninstall option.)

2. Save the uninstaller to your computer.

3. Close any browser or program that uses Adobe Flash. (This includes instant messengers and games.)

4. Find the uninstaller you saved on your computer. Double-click and follow prompts. Allow the program to make changes to your computer.

5. Go to Start and choose Run. Copy and paste "C:\Windows\ system32\Macromed\Flash" into the Open box.

6. Delete all files in folder.

7. Repeat steps 5 and 6 for:

   a. C:\Windows\SysWOW64\Macromed\Flash

   b. %appdata%\Adobe\Flash Player

   c. %appdata%\Macromedia\Flash Player

8. Restart your computer to complete uninstallation.

If you are using a Mac:

1. Determine what OS X your Mac is running. To do this, Click the Apple icon on the top left of your screen and then choose About This Mac. Write down the version number.

2. Visit https://helpx.adobe.com and search Uninstall Flash Player for Mac OS.

3. Scroll down to Step Two and download the Flash Uninstaller for your Mac operating system.

4. The uninstaller will now be in the Downloads folder of your browser. Open that folder and double-click the uninstaller.

5. Open the uninstaller and then choose Uninstall.

6. You will be prompted to close all of your open browsers.

7. Once your browsers are closed, Flash will uninstall. You will receive a message when the uninstallation is complete. Click Done.

8. Lastly, delete these directories:

   a. <home directory>/Library/Preferences/Macromedia/ Flash\ Player

   b. <home directory>/Library/Caches/Adobe/Flash\ Player

9. Restart computer.

Disable Flash in Your Browsers

You're almost done, but before you can be free of Flash, you need to disable the plugin from browsers that contain them (Chrome, Internet Explorer). Note you need to do this for ALL the browsers downloaded on your machine, not just the one or two that you use. Leaving Flash enabled on a browser can lead to malware and hacks even if you do not use the browser.[24]

Google Chrome (Windows and Mac)

1. Open your Google Chrome browser.

2. Type: chrome://plugins/ into the browser and click Enter.

3. Find Adobe Flash Player on your list of plugins and click Disable.

Internet Explorer

1. Open Internet Explorer browser.

2. Click on the gear icon in the top-right corner.

3. Click Manage add-ons. Click Show and Choose All add-ons.

4. Scroll down and find Shockwave Flash Object and click Disable.

Microsoft Edge (Windows 10)

1. Open Edge.

2. Click the Menu button and then click Settings.

3. Toggle Use Adobe Flash Player to off.

If you do run into a situation where you need Flash, you can enable it in your browser.

Uninstall or Disable Java

Oracle's Java software also comes under frequent attack and needs security holes plugged. Many people don't even know if they have Java and most likely don't need the program. We recommend uninstalling Java if you do not use it. If you think you will need the program, you should disable it when not in use.[25]

Uninstall Java

Windows computers:

1. Click Start.

2. Click Control Panel.

3. Select Programs and Features.

4. Scroll down and find Java. Click once.

5. Click Uninstall button near the top left.

Mac computers:

1. Open Finder.

2. Choose Applications.

3. In the Search box, enter: JavaAppletPlugin.plugin.

4. Right-click on the plugin and choose Move to Trash.

Disable Java in Browsers

Google Chrome:
1. Open your Google Chrome browser.

2. Type: chrome://plugins/ into the browser and click Enter.

3. Find Java on your list of plugins and click Disable.

Internet Explorer: (Note: Edge does not support Java.)
1. Open Internet Explorer browser.

2. Click on the gear icon in the top-right corner.

3. Click Manage add-ons. Click Show and Choose All add-ons.

4. Scroll down and find Java and click Disable.

Mozilla Firefox:
1. Open Firefox browser.

2. Click the icon with three lines at the top-right corner.

3. Click Add-ons.

4. Click Plugins.

5. Scroll down and find Java. Click Disable/Never Activate.

Unsupported Version of Internet Explorer

As of 2016, Microsoft stopped supporting older versions of Internet Explorer including Internet Explorer 7, 8, 9, 10. Microsoft recommended that everyone using Internet Explorer updated to IE 11 or Microsoft Edge (offered on Windows 10). Computers running older versions of IE remain vulnerable to security holes and zero-day attacks as Microsoft no longer sends updates.

(Microsoft also no longer supports the Windows XP operating system.)

Even if you do not use Internet Explorer but are a Windows user or have it installed on your machine, you must update to the newest version. Hackers can still exploit holes on the older version sitting on your machine.[26]

iTunes

A report by security firm Secunia found that almost 50 percent of iTunes users are running an outdated version of the music program. Many refrain from updating iTunes because they don't want to adapt to a new design of the music store or their playlists. But iTunes updates contain more than cosmetic changes: Secunia said that iTunes had over a hundred security vulnerabilities in an eleven-month period. One iTunes vulnerability allowed Mac users to compromise other accounts on that computer. Another flaw gave hackers the opportunity to intercept users' passwords. You can't ignore the "Update" box that pops up every time you open your iTunes account. Ignoring them puts you at risk.[27]

To make sure you run the newest version of iTunes, open iTunes on your computer and click iTunes on the menu bar. Then select Check for Updates to start the process.

Postponing Restart

To stop your Windows 10 computer from restarting at inopportune times following an update, you can set your computer to install updates at a certain time. Go to Start, Settings, Update & Security, then click Advanced Settings. There you can select Install updates automatically at a certain time every day. This allows your computer to update and restart in the middle of the night when you are sleeping. Just be sure to save your work before going to bed.

To set your Mac to automatically check for and install updates at a certain time, you need to check for updates manually once at that time. For example, if one night at 10:30 p.m. you go to System Preferences, Software Update, and click Check Now, your Mac will check for and install updates at 10:30 p.m. in the future as long as your computer is on. If you want to set the updates for even later but don't want to stay up, you can trick your Mac by changing the Date and Time to the time of your choice and then doing the above steps.

Estimated Completion Time: Less than thirty minutes

Action Step #15:
Back Up Your Files

As we learned in chapter 15, you must add to your cybersecurity plan the important task of backing up your data. The rule of three states that you should have copies of your data in three places: on your computer where you created or saved the original files, a physical backup (external hard drive), and a virtual backup you can access anywhere (cloud storage). Follow these guidelines to get your backup plan going:

- **Your Local Copies:** The first leg of the rule involves your saved files, operating system, and software that you stored on your computer or device. Anything you save on those will be copied to the other legs of the rule of three—cloud and physical backup.

- **Your Online (Cloud) Backup:** The second leg requires keeping copies of your files "in the cloud," on one of the many online storage sites such as Dropbox, Apple's iCloud Drive, Google Drive, and Microsoft OneDrive. These services provide one great advantage: When you save your files to these drives, they create a local copy and a backup copy that automatically sync to the cloud and your other connected devices and computers. That means you can get your current files on your desktop, laptop, tablet, and smartphone. Plus, the services have "versioning" that tracks down earlier copies of your files if needed. These backup programs are safe, convenient, and offer free storage up to certain limits. No excuses for not making a cloud service part of your backup plan!

Most cloud services offer free storage up to a certain amount. Above the free limit, you'll pay a small monthly fee. If you have a lot of data or run a business, you'll want to research your options for this mission-critical task. When you do choose a cloud service, make sure to protect your account with a strong password and turn on two-step verification.

- **Your Physical Backup:** The third leg entails copying your files to an external disk or hard drive—a fast, easy, and cheap action. External hard drives attach to your computer to back up your files and start at about $50. In addition to regularly copying your files, experts suggest you make a one-time physical copy of your operating systems and other software, called a "full image" backup.[28] Those files won't be part of your daily or weekly backup, but you'll have them to restore your computer to full strength in the event that something happens to your hard drive. For Macs and Windows, just plug in the machines and follow the on-screen prompts. Remember to back up your smartphones and tablets, too.

When and How Much to Back Up

When you have cloud storage, you can save your local files under your cloud drive icon in your Favorites area on your computer. Once you move your folders and files to that location and continue to work and save from there, you've got your local and online backup covered in one spot. Now you just need to schedule your physical backup using an external drive. In essence, the physical backup becomes the backup of your backup. Unless you operate a business, you should make a physical copy weekly. Once you have one full-image copy of your machine's files and software, you can set the external drive to copy only recently added and updated files. That will speed the backup process.

Estimated Completion Time: Less than fifteen minutes

Paying the Ransom

If you are infected with ransomware and don't have a backup, you may need to pay the ransom to get your files back. To do so, you need to understand the world of bitcoin. (Note: Bitcoin is an unregulated currency. There is very little protection in the case of theft and not all banks will take part in bitcoin transactions.)

First, you'll need to install a bitcoin wallet on your computer. This acts as your digital-currency bank account. You can download and install the wallet at bitcoin.org/en/download. Other wallets are available, but this is the official one.

Next, decide how you want to obtain your bitcoin. If you are not pressed for time, more options are available. For example, you can use a website like coinbase.com to link to your bank account and transfer money. Once the transaction goes through, the currency will appear in your wallet. The service charges a fee, and it takes a few days.

If you need coins right away, you'll have to use an exchange. These sites, such as LocalBitcoins.com, will put you in contact with bitcoin buyers and sellers in your area. You will have to meet in person to exchange your cash for bitcoins, so you should be careful.

You can also find a bitcoin ATM in your area through CoinDesk .com. You can visit these ATMs and exchange your cash for bitcoins.

However you decide to obtain bitcoins, you'll need to know your wallet information and the most recent dollar-to-bitcoin conversion rate, which changes frequently. Check right before the transaction so you know you are getting enough bitcoins to cover the ransom.

Once you have your currency, follow the ransomware payment instructions. You'll enter the recipient's information through your bitcoin wallet and then send the currency to the fraudster's untraceable wallet. Once you hit Send, the transaction is irreversible. Please note, poorly designed ransomware occasionally will leave your computer encrypted even after you've paid the ransom. Consult a computer tech if that happens.[29]

Action Step #16:
Examine Message for Signs of Fraud

If you're uncertain about the identity of an email's sender, you should view the full email header or the email properties. Doing so will give you even more information about where the email came from.[30] Follow the instructions below for your email provider:

- **Microsoft Outlook** (Windows App): Open the email message. Choose File, Info, and then Properties. At the bottom you will see a section called Internet headers. This will give you more information about the sender.

- **Microsoft Outlook** (Webmail): Open the email message. Depending on the version of Outlook you are using, either click on the Message Details icon (an image of an envelope and a letter) or click the ellipsis next to the Reply and Forward buttons. From there, select View Message Details. Note: If you are using Microsoft Outlook Webmail 2007, you will not be able to view the full header.

- **Gmail**: Open the email. To get the shorter Internet header, click the small arrow next to "to me." This will show "from the sender" info and the reply-to address. To get the longer header, click the arrow next to the Reply button and choose Show Original.

- **Yahoo**: After opening the email, click the gear icon at the top of the message. Choose View Full Header.

- **AOL**: Open the message and choose View Message Source from the Action menu near the Reply button.

- **iCloud**: Double-click the email to open it in a new window, then click the gear icon and click Show Long Headers.

Phishing Detection Features in Your Browser

In addition to knowing how to dissect a suspicious email and examine the message for signs of fraud, your web browser settings provide some important phishing-detection features that boost your security, too. Popular Internet browsers such as Chrome, Firefox, Safari, Internet Explorer, and Microsoft's new Edge can help us fend off phishing attacks. The latest versions of these browsers have built-in anti-phishing features turned on by default. They will alert you to known phishing websites before you view a dangerous page. But you cannot exclusively rely on browsers, because they can only help you with known phishing sites, not new ones. (So keep practicing the EMAIL Rule.) Some guidance on where to check your browser to confirm or turn on phishing-detection settings:

- **Google Chrome**: Click the Menu button, then choose Settings, and then Advanced Settings. Scroll down to see Privacy and check "Protect you and your device from dangerous sites."

- **Internet Explorer**: Click Tools from your browser. Next, select Phishing Filter and Turn On Automatic Website Checking. Then check Turn on Phishing Filter.

- **Microsoft Edge:** Open your browser and click the Menu button. Select Advanced Settings and then Turn SmartScreen Filter on.

- **Mozilla Firefox:** Click the Menu button at the top-right corner. Next, click Security. Under General, check "Warn me when sites try to install add-ons," "Block reported attack sites," and "Block reported web forgeries."

- **Safari:** Go to Settings and then Safari. Check Fraudulent Website Warning.

Estimated Completion Time: Less than ten minutes

Action Step #17:
Inspect Links to Confirm Fraud

Knowing how to inspect potentially dangerous links will help you avoid succumbing to phishing frauds on your laptop or computer. But spotting suspicious links that arrive on your mobile devices requires extreme caution.

SMiShing

Increasingly, phishers target smartphones and tablets by sending text messages with malware links, a fraud called "SMiShing," a mash-up of phishing and the technical acronym for a text message, SMS. Mobile text links don't work the same way that computer and laptop links work. You can't hover over the link to inspect its true origin, which makes text messages troublesome. That means that when you suddenly receive a text link from your phone company, for example, you cannot determine its legitimacy. Don't click. Instead, call the company directly or visit its website on your own to pursue the matter. As a rule, when it comes to mobile text messages, question anyone asking you to follow a link.

Vishing

Some phishers rely on less-technical schemes to get your personal information. One scam called "Vishing" (voice plus phishing) happens when a fraudster calls you impersonating a legitimate business or organization and asks for your personal information so they can later use it to compromise your identity or financial accounts.[31] If you get an unsolicited call and doubt its legitimacy, ask to call them back. Hang up the phone, look up the company's customer service number, and call that number directly.

Action Step #18:
Take Control of Your Cybersecurity Now

Many of the "extras" offered in identity protection services can be done on your own for free or very little cost. We've covered most of them in the body of this book, such as text/email alerts and setting up a Security Freeze. Additional steps you can take to protect your identity include:

- **Lost or stolen wallet protection:** Many of these services charge a monthly fee for assistance in closing bank and credit accounts if your wallet is lost or stolen. You can cancel your own lost or stolen cards for free by contacting the bank or credit card company directly. We also recommend only carrying the cards you need.

- **Reduce pre-approved credit card offers:** You can opt out of unsolicited mail and pre-approved credit card and insurance options on your own for free. Sign up for the Do Not Mail list at www.dmachoice.org. Opt out of prescreened credit card and insurance options at www.optoutprescreen.com. While you're at it, add yourself to the Do Not Call list at www.donotcall.gov.[32]

- **Annual Credit Report:** Some of the higher-tier services offer access to an annual credit report from one of the major credit bureaus. However, everyone has access to one free credit report from each of the bureaus per year. To access yours, go to www.annualcreditreport.com.[33]

Endnotes

Introduction

1. "Phishing: How Many Take the Bait?," *Get Cyber Safe*, March 4, 2015, http://www.getcybersafe.gc.ca/cnt/rsrcs/nfgrphcs/nfgrphcs-2012-10-11-en.aspx.

2. Jeff Goldman, "Almost 100 Billion Spam E-mails Sent Daily in Q1 2013," *eSecurity Planet*, May 3, 2013, http://www.esecurityplanet.com/network-security/almost-100-billion-spam-e-mails-sent-daily-in-q1-2013.html.

3. P.W. Singer and Allan Friedman, *Cybersecurity and Cyberwarfare: What Everyone Needs to Know* (New York: Oxford University Press, 2014), p. 4.

4. Michelle Fox, "Cyberattacks Grave National Security Threat: WH Advisor," *CNBC*, February 13, 2015, http://www.cnbc.com/2015/02/13/cyberattacks-grave-national-security-threat-wh-advisor.html.

5. David E. Sanger and Nicole Perlroth, "Iranian Hackers Attack State Dept. via Social Media Accounts," the *New York Times*, November 24, 2015, http://www.nytimes.com/2015/11/25/world/middleeast/iran-hackers-cyberespionage-state-department-social-media.html.

Part I: Secrecy

Increase Your Stealth, Boost Your Security

1. Bob Al-Greene, "Did You Know 144.8 Billion Emails Are Sent Every Day?," *Mashable*, November 27, 2012, http://mashable.com/2012/11/27/email-stats-infographic/#gZ8ZconZX8qN.

2. Al Pascual, "2014 Identity Fraud Report: Card Data Breaches and Inadequate Consumer Password Habits Fuel Disturbing Fraud Trends," Javelin Strategy, February 5, 2014, https://www.javelinstrategy.com/coverage-area/2014-identity-fraud-report-card-data-breaches-and-inadequate-consumer-password-habits.

3. Donna Tapellini, "70 Million Americans Report Stolen Data," *Consumer Reports*, May 7, 2015, http://www.consumerreports.org/cro/news/2015/05/70-million-americans-report-stolen-data/index.htm

4. "ITRC Data Breach Reports, December 31, 2015," Identity Theft Resource Center, December 31, 2015, http://www.idtheftcenter.org/images/breach/DataBreachReports_2015.pdf.

5. "Data Breaches," Identity Theft Resource Center, June 16, 2016, http://www.idtheftcenter.org/index.php/id-theft/data-breaches.html.

6. Brian Krebs, "Exploring the Market for Stolen Passwords," *Krebs on Security*, December 26, 2012, http://krebsonsecurity.com/2012/12/exploring-the-market-for-stolen-passwords/.

7. Brian Krebs, "The Value of a Hacked Email Account," *Krebs on Security*, June 10, 2013, http://krebsonsecurity.com/2013/06/the-value-of-a-hacked-email-account/.

8. "2015 Identity Fraud Study," Javelin Strategy & Research, 2015.

Chapter One: Your Email Address Is the Key to Your Digital Life: It Shouldn't Be Everywhere!

1. Herbert H. Thompson, "How I Stole Someone's Identity," *Scientific American*, August 18, 2008, http://www.scientificamerican.com/article/anatomy-of-a-social-hack/.

2. Robert Siciliano, "Connecting the Dots—How Your Digital Life Affects Identity Theft and Financial Loss," *Robert Siciliano*, July 13, 2013, http://robertsiciliano.com/blog/2013/07/13/connecting-the-dots-how-your-digital-life-affects-identity-theft-and-financial-loss/.

3. Brian Krebs, "The Value of a Hacked Email Account."

4. Adam Levin, "The Simple Email Trick that Could Protect Your Identity," *Credit.com*, January 29, 2015, http://blog.credit.com/2015/01/the-simple-email-trick-that-could-protect-your-identity-107365/.

Chapter Two: Love Your Passwords, Lose Weight, and Beat the Password Paradox

1. Mauricio Estrella, "How a Password Changed My Life," *Medium*, May 14, 2014, https://medium.com/the-lighthouse/how-a-password-changed-my-life-7af5d5f28038#.aczyxpt5a.

2. "Consumer Password Worst Practices," the Imperva Application Defense Center (ADC), January 21, 2010, http://www.imperva.com/docs/wp_consumer_password_worst_practices.pdf.

3. Bruce Schneier, "Passwords Are Not Broken, but How We Choose Them Sure Is," *Schneier on Security*, November 13, 2008, https://www.schneier.com/essays/archives/2008/11/passwords_are_not_br.html.

4. Michah Lee, "Passphrases That You Can Memorize—But That Even the NSA Guys Can't Guess," *The Intercept*, March 26, 2015, https://theintercept.com/2015/03/26/passphrases-can-memorize-attackers-cant-guess/.

5. Marjan Ghazvininejad and Kevin Knight, "How to Memorize a Random 60-Bit String," Information Sciences Institute, Department of Computer Science, University of Southern California, http://www.isi.edu/natural-language/mt/memorize-random-60.pdf.

6. Graham Cluley, "Outlook Webmail Passwords Restricted to 16 Chars—How Does That Compare with Yahoo and Gmail?," *Naked Security by Sophos*, August 2, 2012, https://nakedsecurity.sophos.com/2012/08/02/maximum-password-length-outlook-yahoo-gmail-compared/.

7. "What Are Gmail's Password Requirements?," *Password Pit*, June 2, 2015, http://www.passwordpit.com/gmail-password-requirements/.

Chapter Three: The Two-Step Process That Stops Hackers

1. James Fallows, "Hacked!," the *Atlantic*, November 2011 Issue, http://www.theatlantic.com/magazine/archive/2011/11/hacked/308673/.

2. Whitson Gordon, "Here's Everywhere You Should Enable Two-Factor Authentication Right Now," *Lifehacker*, December 10, 2013, http://lifehacker.com/5938565/heres-everywhere-you-should-enable-two-factor-authentication-right-now.

Chapter Four: Too Many Passwords and the Unbreakable Solution

1. Elizabeth Weise, "Starbucks Customers' Mobile Accounts Breached by Thieves," *USA Today*, May 16, 2015, http://www.usatoday.com/story/tech/2015/05/15/starbucks-gift-card-hack/27370491/.

2. Chris Hoffman, "Why You Should Use a Password Manager and How to Get Started," *How-to Geek*, September 9, 2015, http://www.howtogeek.com/141500/why-you-should-use-a-password-manager-and-how-to-get-started/.

Chapter Five: The Danger of Free Public Wi-Fi: It's a Honeypot for Hackers

1. Mohit Kumar, "Three Politicians Hacked Using Unsecured Wi-Fi Network," *The Hacker News*, July 11, 2015, http://thehackernews.com/2015/07/unsecure-public-wifi-hacking.html.

2. Maurits Martijn, "Here's Why Public Wi-Fi Is a Public Health Hazard," *Medium*, October 14, 2014, https://medium.com/matter/heres-why-public-wifi-is-a-public-health-hazard-dd5b8dcb55e6#.87gvat26q.

3. Alan Henry, "Why You Should Start Using a VPN (and How to Choose the Best One for Your Needs)," *Lifehacker*, September 5, 2012, http://lifehacker.com/5940565/why-you-should-start-using-a-vpn-and-how-to-choose-the-best-one-for-your-needs.

Chapter Six: "Good Fences Make Good Neighbors" Applies to Your Home Wi-Fi Network

1. Roger Grimes, "How to Stop Wi-Fi Hackers Cold," *InfoWorld*, May 26, 2015, http://www.infoworld.com/article/2925636/security/how-to-stop-wi-fi-hackers-cold.html.

2. Jason Fitzpatrick, "HTG Explains: The Difference Between WEP, WPA, and WPA2 Wireless Encryption (and Why It Matters)," *How-to Geek*, July 16, 2013, http://www.howtogeek.com/167783/htg-explains-the-difference-between-wep-wpa-and-wpa2-wireless-encryption-and-why-it-matters/.

3. Chris Hoffman, "Wi-Fi Protected Setup (WPS) is Insecure: Here's Why You Should Disable It," *How-to Geek*, November 24, 2013, http://www.howtogeek.com/176124/wi-fi-protected-setup-wps-is-insecure-heres-why-you-should-disable-it/.

4. Jennifer Valentino-Devries, " Rarely Patched Software Bugs in Home Routers Cripple Security," the *Wall Street Journal*, January 18, 2016, http://www.wsj.com/articles/rarely-patched-software-bugs-in-home-routers-cripple-security-1453136285.

Chapter Seven: Protect Your Phone and Tablet: Track Them like a Bounty Hunter

1. Amy Gahran, "Most Finders of Lost Phones Try to Access Personal Data, Survey Finds," *CNN*, March 20, 2012, http://www.cnn.com/2012/03/20/tech/mobile/lost-smartphones-security/.

2. "Number of Apps Available in Leading App Stores as of July 2015," Statista, http://www.statista.com/statistics/276623/number-of-apps-available-in-leading-app-stores/.

3. Donna Tapellini, "Smart Phone Thefts Rose to 3.1 million in 2013," *Consumer Reports*, May 28, 2014, http://www.consumerreports.org/cro/news/2014/04/smart-phone-thefts-rose-to-3-1-million-last-year/index.htm

4. Biz Carson, "The Potentially Life-Saving iPhone Feature You Probably Didn't Notice," *Slate*, December 1, 2015, http://www.slate.com/blogs/business_insider/2015/12/01/a_hidden_health_app_on_your_iphone_can_make_your_emergency_medical_information.html.

Chapter Eight: How to Stop Identity Theft on Facebook and Other Social Media

1. Tom Rawstorne, "My Identity Was Stolen on Facebook," *Daily Mail*, July 27, 2007, http://www.dailymail.co.uk/femail/article-471321/My-identity-stolen-Facebook.html.

2. Julia Greenberg, "1 Billion People Used Facebook on Monday," *Wired*, August 27, 2015, http://www.wired.com/2015/08/1-billion-people-used-facebook-monday/.

3. "Number of Monthly Active Twitter Users Worldwide from 1st Quarter 2010 to 3rd Quarter 2015 (in millions)," *Statista*, http://www.statista.com/statistics/282087/number-of-monthly-active-twitter-users/.

4. "Instagram Today: 500 Million Windows to the World," Instagram, June, 21, 2016, http://blog.instagram.com/post/146255204757/160621-news.

5. Ken Lewis, "How Social Media Networks Facilitate Identity Theft and Fraud," Entrepreneurs' Organization, https://www.eonetwork.org/octane-magazine/special-features/social-media-networks-facilitate-identity-theft-fraud.

6. "2012 Norton Cybercrime Report," Norton by Symantec, 2012, http://now-static.norton.com/now/en/pu/images/Promotions/2012/cybercrimeReport/2012_Norton_Cybercrime_Report_Master_FINAL_050912.pdf.

Part II: Omniscience

Your Brain against the Hackers

1. Bruce Schneier, "The Psychology of Security (Part 1)," *Schneier on Security*, January 18, 2008, https://www.schneier.com/essays/archives/2008/01/the_psychology_of_se.html.

2. Mirana Hitti, "Car Crashes Kill 40,000 in U.S. Every Year," *Fox News*, February 3, 2005, http://www.foxnews.com/story/2005/02/03/car-crashes-kill-40000-in-us-every-year.html.

3. Bruce Schneier, "The Psychology of Security (Part 1)."

Chapter Nine: Track Your Money in Motion, Just Like the Banks Do

1. Michael Finney, "Woman's Debit Card Suspended Due to Target Breach," *ABC 7*, January 14, 2014, http://abc7news.com/archive/9393709/.

2. Zach Whittaker, "These Companies Lost Your Data in 2015's Biggest Hacks, Breaches," *ZDNet*, November 30, 2015, http://www.zdnet.com/pictures/biggest-hacks-security-data-breaches-2015/.

3. "Lost or Stolen Credit, ATM, and Debit Cards," Federal Trade Commission, August 2012, http://www.consumer.ftc.gov/articles/0213-lost-or-stolen-credit-atm-and-debit-cards.

Chapter Ten: A Simple Way to Stop Identity Theft and Protect Your Good Name

1. Elaine Wilson, "Identity Theft—One Military Retiree's Story," *Army News Service*, http://usmilitary.about.com/od/payandbenefits/a/idtheft.htm.

2. Blake Ellis, "Identity Fraud Hits New Victim Every Two Seconds," *CNN Money*, February 6, 2014, http://money.cnn.com/2014/02/06/pf/identity-fraud/.

3. Brian Krebs, "How I Learned to Stop Worrying and Embrace the Security Freeze," *Krebs on Security*, June 8, 2015, http://krebsonsecurity.com/2015/06/how-i-learned-to-stop-worrying-and-embrace-the-security-freeze/.

4. Brian Krebs, "Are Credit Monitoring Services Worth It?," *Krebs on Security*, March 19, 2014, http://krebsonsecurity.com/2014/03/are-credit-monitoring-services-worth-it/.

5. "Nearly 1 in 4 Americans Have Never Checked Their Credit Report," *Credit.com*, April 26, 2013, http://blog.credit.com/2013/04/nearly-1-in-4-americans-have-never-checked-their-credit-report-65892/.

Chapter Eleven: One Thing Parents Must Do to Protect Their Children from Identity Theft

1. Barbara Whitaker, "Never Too Young to Have Your Identity Stolen," the *New York Times*, July 21, 2007, http://www.nytimes.com/2007/07/21/business/21id-theft.html?pagewanted=all&_r=1&mtrref=undefined.

2. Geraldine Sealey, "Child ID Theft Can Go Unnoticed for Years," *ABC News*, September 12, 2003, http://abcnews.go.com/US/story?id=90257&page=1.

3. "Child Identity Theft," Federal Trade Commission, August 2012, http://www.consumer.ftc.gov/articles/0040-child-identity-theft.

4. Brian Krebs, "The Lowdown on Freezing Your Kid's Credit," *Krebs on Security*, January 20, 2016, http://krebsonsecurity.com/2016/01/the-lowdown-on-freezing-your-kids-credit/.

5. "Child Identity Theft," Federal Trade Commission.

Chapter Twelve: How to Spot ATM Skimmers and Foil Identity Thieves

1. "Man Indicted in Idaho Card Skimming Scheme," *InstaKey*, February 5, 2014, http://www.instakey.com/currentnews/man-indicted-in-idaho-card-skimming-scheme/.

2. "Card Skimming," *Webopedia*, http://www.webopedia.com/TERM/C/card_skimming.html.

3. Brian Krebs, "Gang Used 3-D Printers for ATM Skimmers," *Krebs on Security*, September 20, 2011, http://krebsonsecurity.com/2011/09/gang-used-3d-printers-for-atm-skimmers/.

4. Justin Pritchard, "Skimming Scams," *About Money*, May 8, 2015, http://banking.about.com/od/securityandsafety/a/skimmers.htm

5. Fahmida Y. Rashid, "How to Spot and Avoid Credit Card Skimmers," *PC Magazine*, October 15, 2014, http://www.pcmag.com/article2/0,2817,2469560,00.asp.

6. "Lost or Stolen Credit, ATM, and Debit Cards," Federal Trade Commission, August 2012, http://www.consumer.ftc.gov/articles/0213-lost-or-stolen-credit-atm-and-debit-cards.

7. Tony Armstrong, "EMV Cards Can't Be Skimmed Like Magstripe Cards," *NerdWallet*, February 3, 2015, https://www.nerdwallet.com/blog/credit-cards/emv-cards-skimmed-magstripe-cards/.

Part III: Mindfulness

Stay Hack-Proofed When Your Brain Says *Click!*

1. Emily Yoffe, "Seeking," *Slate*, August 12, 2009, http://www.slate.com/articles/health_and_science/science/2009/08/seeking.html.

2. Nathan Chandler, "What Is the History of the Remote Control?," *How Stuff Works*, March 3, 2011, http://science.howstuffworks.com/innovation/repurposed-inventions/history-of-remote-control.htm.

3. Emily Yoffe, "Seeking."

4. "Phishing in the Dark," *McAfee Business Blog*, August 21, 2013, https://blogs.mcafee.com/business/phishing-in-the-dark/.

5. "A Brief History of NSP and the Internet," National Science Foundation, http://www.nsf.gov/news/special_reports/cyber/internet.jsp.

6. "Gartner Says 6.4 Billion Connected 'Things' Will Be in Use in 2016, Up 30 Percent from 2015," Gartner, November 10, 2015, http://www.gartner.com/newsroom/id/3165317.

7. Sarah Bogarty, " Internet-Connected Devices Surpass Half a Billion in U.S. Homes, According to the NPD Group," The NPD Group, March 18, 2013, https://www.npd.com/wps/portal/npd/us/news/press-releases/internet-connected-devices-surpass-half-a-billion-in-u-s-homes-according-to-the-npd-group/.

8. Bob Al-Greene, "Did You Know 144.8 Billion Emails Are Sent Every Day?."

9. Virginia Harrison and Jose Pagliery, "Nearly 1 Million New Malware Threats Released Every Day," *CNN Money*, April 14, 2015, http://money.cnn.com/2015/04/14/technology/security/cyber-attack-hacks-security/.

10. "OODA Loops: Understanding the Decision Cycle," *Mind Tools*, https://www.mindtools.com/pages/article/newTED_78.htm.

11. Mihaly Csikszentmihalyi, *Flow: The Psychology of Optimal Experience*, Harper Perennial Modern Classics, 2008.

12. Sensei Kipp Ryodo Hawley, "Mindfulness," *Zen Mindfulness: The 3-step Zen Method*, http://www.zenmindfulness.com/.

13. Iulia Ion, Rob Reeder, and Sunny Consolvo, "'…No One Can Hack My Mind': Comparing Expert and Non-Expert Security Practices," July 2015 Symposium

on Usable Privacy and Security, July 2015, https://www.usenix.org/system/files/conference/soups2015/soups15-paper-ion.pdf.

Chapter Thirteen: The One Software Program You Must Know Well

1. Michael Sperry, "Professional Blogger Shares Her 'Scareware' Story," *Vimeo*, May 28, 2011, https://vimeo.com/24365075.

2. "Classic Malware," *Panda Security*, http://www.pandasecurity.com/homeusers/security-info/classic-malware/.

3. Maria Garnaeva, Jornt van der Wiel, Denis Makrushin, Anton Ivanov, and Yury Namestnikov, "Kaspersky Security Bulletin 2015," Kaspersky Lab, December 15, 2015, https://securelist.com/analysis/kaspersky-security-bulletin/73038/kaspersky-security-bulletin-2015-overall-statistics-for-2015/.

4. Robert Siciliano, "What Is a 'Drive-By' Download?," *McAfee Consumer Blog*, April 2, 2013, https://blogs.mcafee.com/consumer/drive-by-download/.

5. "Microsoft Security Intelligence Report," Microsoft, vol. 19, January-June 2015, https://www.microsoft.com/security/sir/default.aspx.

6. Neil J. Rubenking, "Why You Need Antivirus Software," *PC Magazine*, December 17, 2014, http://securitywatch.pcmag.com/security-software/330459-why-you-need-antivirus-software.

Chapter Fourteen: What Security Experts ALWAYS Do and Why You Should Do the Same

1. Brian Krebs, "A Month Without Adobe Flash Player," *Krebs on Security*, June 23, 2015, http://krebsonsecurity.com/2015/06/a-month-without-adobe-flash-player/.

2. Iulia Ion, Rob Reeder, Sunny Consolvo, "'…No One Can Hack My Mind': Comparing Expert and Non-Expert Security Practices."

3. Linda Summers, "Survey Finds Nearly Half of Consumers Fail to Upgrade Software Regularly and One Quarter of Consumers Don't Know Why To Update Software," *Skype Big Blog*, July 23, 2012, http://blogs.skype.com/2012/07/23/intl-tech-upgrade-week/.

4. James A. Lewis, "Raising the Bar for Cybersecurity," Center for Strategic & International Studies, February 12, 2013, http://csis.org/files/publication/130212_Lewis_RaisingBarCybersecurity.pdf.

5. Robert Siciliano, "What Is a 'Drive-By' Download?," *McAfee Consumer Blog*, April 2, 2013, https://blogs.mcafee.com/consumer/drive-by-download/.

6. Taylor Armstrong, "Why Users Don't Often Upgrade Software When They Should," *CSO Online*, July 30, 2012, http://www.csoonline.com/article/2132061/

security-awareness/why-users-don-t-often-upgrade-software-when-they-should.html

7. Chris Hoffman, "Defend Your Windows PC from Junkware: 5 Lines of Defense," *How-to Geek*, September 13, 2014, http://www.howtogeek.com/196259/defend-your-windows-pc-from-junkware-5-lines-of-defense/

8. Chris Hoffman, "Why You Need to Install Windows Updates Automatically," *How-to Geek*, November 17, 2014, http://www.howtogeek.com/howto/31204/why-do-application-installs-make-you-reboot-and-close-other-apps/.

9. Roman Loyola, "How to Adjust OS X's Software Update," *Macworld*, http://www.macworld.com/article/1164882/how_to_adjust_os_x_s_software_update.html.

10. Chris Hoffman, "Why You Need to Install Windows Updates Automatically."

11. Brian Krebs, "Flash, Java Patches Fix Critical Holes," *Krebs on Security*, October 20, 2015, http://krebsonsecurity.com/2015/10/flash-java-patches-fix-critical-holes/.

12. "What does it mean if Windows isn't supported?," Microsoft, http://windows.microsoft.com/en-us/windows/help/what-does-end-of-support-mean.

Chapter Fifteen: How to Guarantee You Never Pay Extortion to Cyber Thieves

1. Aarti Shahani, "Ransomware: When Hackers Lock Your Files, to Pay or Not to Pay?," *National Public Radio*, December 8, 2014, http://www.npr.org/sections/alltechconsidered/2014/12/08/366849122/ransomware-when-hackers-lock-your-files-to-pay-or-not-to-pay.

2. Aarti Shahani, "Ransomware: When Hackers Lock Your Files, to Pay or Not to Pay?."

3. Scott Hanselman, "The Computer Backup Rule of Three," *Scott Hanselman Blog*, November 14, 2012, http://www.hanselman.com/blog/TheComputer-BackupRuleOfThree.aspx.

4. Anand Khanse, "What to Do After a Ransomware Attack on Your Windows Computer?," *The Windows Club*, April 19, 2016, http://www.thewindowsclub.com/what-to-do-after-ransomware-attack.

Chapter Sixteen: Hackers Never Sleep: Spot the Phisher's Mind Tricks (Ten-Second EMAIL Rule, Part One)

1. Lorenzo Franceschi-Bicchierai, "'Teens' Who Hacked CIA Director Also Hit White House Official," *Motherboard*, January 18, 2016, http://motherboard.vice.com/read/teens-who-hacked-cia-director-also-hit-white-house-official.

2. Bob Al-Greene, " Did You Know 144.8 Billion Emails Are Sent Every Day?"

3. Virginia Harrison and Jose Pagliery, "Nearly 1 million new malware threats released every day," *CNN Money*, April 14, 2015, http://money.cnn.com/2015/04/14/technology/security/cyber-attack-hacks-security/.

4. "Welcome to Phishing.org," *Phishing.org*, http://www.phishing.org/.

5. "What Is Social Engineering?," *Security Through Education*, http://www.social-engineer.org/about/.

6. Alan Henry, "How Spammers Spoof Your Email Address (and How to Protect Yourself)," *Lifehacker*, May 21, 2014, http://lifehacker.com/how-spammers-spoof-your-email-address-and-how-to-prote-1579478914.

7. "Identifying fraudulent 'phishing' email," Apple Support, June 1, 2015, https://support.apple.com/en-us/HT204759.

Chapter Seventeen: The Phisher's Seduction: He Hooks with the Link (Ten-Second EMAIL Rule, Part Two)

1. Jane Corbin, "A Mysterious Email and a Split-Second Mistake: That's All it Took for Internet Gangsters to Hijack My Life…," *Daily Mail*, January 15, 2010, http://www.dailymail.co.uk/news/article-1243634/A-mysterious-email-split-second-mistake-Thats-took-internet-gangsters-hijack-life-.html.

2. Fahmida Y. Rashid, "How to Recognize and Avoid Phishing Emails and Links," *PC Magazine*, November 14, 2013, http://securitywatch.pcmag.com/spam/317892-how-to-recognize-and-avoid-phishing-emails-and-links.

3. Brian Posey, "10 Tips for Spotting a Phishing Email," *TechRepublic*, October 15, 2015, http://www.techrepublic.com/blog/10-things/10-tips-for-spotting-a-phishing-email/.

4. Office of Information Security, "How Can I Tell if a Website Is Secure?," Northeastern University, http://www.northeastern.edu/securenu/how-can-i-tell-if-a-website-is-secure/.

Chapter Eighteen: LifeLock and the Question: Whom Should You Trust to Protect Your Identity? (Psst, Look in the Mirror.)

1. Ebarle et al. v. LifeLock, Inc., California Northern District Court Case No. 3: 15 (2015).

2. Federal Trade Commission v. LifeLock, Inc., 2015 Ariz. Case No. 2:10 (2015).

3. Sue Chang, "LifeLock Slides as Founder Todd Davis Resigns as CEO," *MarketWatch*, January 20, 2016, http://www.marketwatch.com/story/lifelock-slides-as-founder-todd-davis-resigns-as-ceo-2016-01-20.

4. Kim Zetter, "LifeLock CEO's Identity Stolen 13 Times," *Wired*, May 18, 2010, https://www.wired.com/2010/05/lifelock-identity-theft/.

5. Colleen Tressler, "LifeLock Agrees to Pay $100 Million for Allegedly Violating FTC Order," Federal Trade Commission, December 17, 2015, https://www.consumer.ftc.gov/blog/lifelock-agrees-pay-100-million-allegedly-violating-ftc-order.

6. "Identity Theft Protection Services," Federal Trade Commission, March 2016, https://www.consumer.ftc.gov/articles/0235-identity-theft-protection-services.

7. "Membership Pricing," LifeLock, 2016, https://www.lifelock.com/.

Chapter Nineteen: Get It Done—Boost Your Cybersecurity Today

1. Ethan Hale, "Goals: The Difference Between Success and Failure," *Fast Company*, http://www.fastcompany.com/1798754/goals-difference-between-success-and-failure.

2. Marie Kondo, *The Life-Changing Magic of Tidying Up* (Berkeley: Ten Speed Press, 2014,) 24.

Hack-Proof Action Guide

1. Alan Henry, "Why You Should Start Using a VPN (and How to Choose the Best One for Your Needs)," *Lifehacker*, September 5, 2012, http://lifehacker.com/5940565/why-you-should-start-using-a-vpn-and-how-to-choose-the-best-one-for-your-needs.

2. Chris Hoffman, "How to Find Your Router's IP Address on Any Computer, Smartphone, or Tablet," *How-to Geek*, November 20, 2015, http://www.howtogeek.com/233952/how-to-find-your-routers-ip-address-on-any-computer-smartphone-or-tablet/.

3. Anthony Domanico, " Change Your Router's Username and Password: How To," *Laptop*, May 3, 2013, http://www.laptopmag.com/articles/change-your-routers-username-and-password-how-to.

4. Becky Waring, "How to Secure Your Wireless Network," *PC World*, April 9, 2007, http://www.pcworld.com/article/130330/article.html.

5. Chris Hoffman, "Wi-Fi Protected Setup (WPS) Is Insecure: Here's Why You Should Disable It," *How-to Geek*, November 24, 2013, http://www.howtogeek.com/176124/wi-fi-protected-setup-wps-is-insecure-heres-why-you-should-disable-it/.

6. Christina Mercer, "How to Update Router Firmware: Improve Network Connectivity by Upgrading Your Firmware," *Techworld*, May 1, 2016, http://www.techworld.com/picture-gallery/personal-tech/how-update-router-firmware-3639485/#5.

7. "What's New in iOS," Apple, http://www.apple.com/ios/whats-new/.

8. Stephen Shankland, "'Reverse Smudge engineering' Foils Android Unlock Security," *CNET*, February 14, 2012, http://www.cnet.com/news/reverse-smudge-engineering-foils-android-unlock-security/.

9. Stephanie Mlot, "Cell Phone Kill Switches Prompt 'Dramatic' Drop in Thefts," *PC Magazine*, February 11, 2015, http://www.pcmag.com/article2/0,2817,2476612,00.asp.

10. Malia Wollan, "Outsmarting Smartphone Thieves," the *New York Times*, May 8, 2013, http://www.nytimes.com/2013/05/09/technology/personaltech/outsmarting-smartphone-thieves.html.

11. Jill Duffy, "How to Add an Emergency Contact to Your Phone's Lock Screen," *PC Magazine*, August 10, 2015, http://www.pcmag.com/article2/0,2817,2489237,00.asp.

12. Erin Lowry, "Consumer Watchdog: Setting Up Credit Card Transaction Text Message Alerts," *Magnify Money*, April 15, 2015, http://www.magnifymoney.com/blog/consumer-watchdog/consumer-watchdog-setting-credit-card-transaction-text-message-alerts666220981.

13. "Nearly 1 in 4 Americans Have Never Checked Their Credit Report," *Credit.com*.

14. Daniel Workman, "Credit File Alerts Canadian Equivalent of U.S. Freeze," *Canada.creditcards.com*, June 19, 2015, http://canada.creditcards.com/credit-card-news/file-alerts-are-Canadas-answer-to-US-report-freezes-1264.php.

15. "Child Identity Theft," Federal Trade Commission, August 2012, https://www.consumer.ftc.gov/articles/0040-child-identity-theft.

16. Heather Morton, "Consumer Report Security Freeze State Laws," National Conference of State Legislatures, March 31, 2016, http://www.ncsl.org/research/financial-services-and-commerce/consumer-report-security-freeze-state-statutes.aspx.

17. Brian Krebs, "The Lowdown on Freezing Your Kid's Credit," *Krebs on Security*, January 20, 2016, http://krebsonsecurity.com/2016/01/the-lowdown-on-freezing-your-kids-credit/.

18. Neil J. Rubenking, "The Best Antivirus Protection for 2016," *PC Magazine*, May 12, 2016, http://www.pcmag.com/article2/0,2817,2372364,00.asp.

19. Chris Hoffman, "How to Run Malwarebytes Alongside Another Antivirus," *How-to Geek*, October 2, 2015, http://www.howtogeek.com/230158/how-to-run-malwarebytes-alongside-another-antivirus/.

20. Benjamin Mayo, "Apple reportedly Cracks Down on Antivirus Apps from iOS App Store, Many Apps Pulled," *9 to 5 Mac*, March 19, 2015, http://9to5mac.com/2015/03/19/apple-app-store-antivirus/.

21. Max Eddy, "17 Android Antivirus Apps Set Perfect Scores," *PC Magazine*, October 13, 2015, http://www.pcmag.com/article2/0,2817,2493066,00.asp.

22. Chris Hoffman, "HTG Explains: Why Every User on Your Computer Should Have Their Own User Account," *How-to Geek*, April 3, 2013, http://www.howtogeek.com/142434/htg-explains-why-every-user-on-your-computer-should-have-their-own-user-account/.

23. Christopher Budd, "Urgent Call to Action: Uninstall QuickTime for Windows Today," *TrendMicro*, April 14, 2016, http://blog.trendmicro.com/urgent-call-action-uninstall-quicktime-windows-today/.

24. Jared Newman, "How to Disable Flash Player: Why Now's a Better Time Than Ever," *PCWorld*, July 13, 2015, http://www.pcworld.com/article/2947381/how-to-disable-flash-player-why-nows-a-better-time-than-ever.html.

25. Brian Krebs, "Good Riddance to Oracle's Java Plugin," *Krebs on Security*, February 2, 2016, http://krebsonsecurity.com/2016/02/good-riddance-to-oracles-java-plugin/.

26. "Support for Older Version of Internet Explorer Ended," Microsoft Support, January 12, 2016, https://www.microsoft.com/en-us/WindowsForBusiness/End-of-IE-support.

27. Jeremy Kirk, "Windows Users Often Forget to Patch Their Apple Programs," *PCWorld*, October 28, 2015, http://www.pcworld.com/article/2998210/security/windows-users-often-forget-to-patch-their-apple-programs.html.

28. Marco Chiappetta, "If We Show You How to Back Up your PC for Free, Will You Finally Do It?," *PCWorld*, February 7, 2014, http://www.pcworld.com/article/2095481/if-we-show-you-how-to-back-up-your-pc-for-free-will-you-finally-do-it.html.

29. "How Can I Buy Bitcoins?," *CoinDesk*, October 28, 2015, http://www.coindesk.com/information/how-can-i-buy-bitcoins/.

30. Jason Faulkner, " HTG Explains: What Can You Find in an Email Header?," *How-to Geek*, March 15, 2012, http://www.howtogeek.com/108205/htg-explains-what-can-you-find-in-an-email-header/.

31. Marie Keyworth, "Vishing and Smishing: The Rise of Social Engineering Fraud," *BBC News*, January 1, 2016, http://www.bbc.com/news/business-35201188.

32. "Prescreened Credit and Insurance Offers," Federal Trade Commission, March 2011, https://www.consumer.ftc.gov/articles/0148-prescreened-credit-and-insurance-offers.

33. "Identity Theft," Federal Trade Commission, May 2015, https://www.consumer.ftc.gov/articles/0005-identity-theft.

Glossary

antivirus software: A program that detects and removes computer viruses by scanning files and downloads on your devices.

back up: A process of copying and saving computer files and data to the cloud or an external system to be used if the original file is lost or damaged.

bitcoin: A type of digital currency that's independent of a central bank, and often used by hackers because of its anonymity.

cloud: Remote servers for storing data that can be accessed via the Internet from any device.

Credit Freeze/Security Freeze: Under this setting (the most secure for your credit file), the credit bureaus will lock your credit file with a PIN. No new credit can be issued in your name unless the freeze is lifted using your PIN.

Credit Monitoring: This service (the least secure for your credit file) tracks your credit daily and alerts you after any changes are made or any new credit is issued.

credit report: A detailed file of an individual's credit history created by the credit bureaus to determine one's creditworthiness.

cybersecurity: Personal behaviors and actions that can protect you from a range of identity-theft frauds and other crimes aimed at stealing your personal information and data.

data breach: A security incident in which criminals steal, copy, view, or use sensitive, protected, or confidential data from a third party.

drive-by-download attack: Malware that can infect your computer or device just from visiting an infected website.

EMV card: Payment cards (Europay, MasterCard, and Visa) on which a consumer's data is stored in a chip rather than a magnetic stripe that can easily be copied. EMV cards encrypt the data differently each time the card is used.

encryption: The process of concealing messages or information with a special code so only others with permission can read them. Encryption creates a private tunnel for information and data to travel through.

external hard drive: A portable storage device that can be connected to your computer. The drive stores selected files.

firewall: A part of a computer system or network that's designed to monitor inward and outward communication between your device, other devices, and the Internet.

firmware: Permanent software that has been programmed into a device.

fraud: A criminal deception carried out with the intention of financial or personal gain.

Fraud Alert: A temporary, less secure setting for your credit file. A note will be placed on your credit file for ninety days to warn potential lenders that you may have been a victim of suspicious activity. Under this setting, extra steps should be taken to verify the legitimacy of a request for new credit before it is issued.

hacker: A person that gains illegal access to a computer network.

hotspot: A device that provides wireless Internet connection in a certain range. Some hotspots may be free to use while others require payment.

hyperlink: A link from one file or webpage to another file or webpage, activated by clicking a highlighted word or image.

identity theft: The illegal use of someone else's personal identifying information such as name, date of birth, or Social Security number in order to steal money, obtain credit, or impersonate the victim.

malware: Malicious software—such as, Trojans, worms, and viruses— that's designed to interfere with a computer's normal functioning.

operating system: The software that supports a computer's basic functions, such as using installed applications.

passcode: A series of numbers or letters that are used to lock your phone or tablet.

password managers: A program that allows you to store your passwords in an encrypted file on your computer or in the cloud.

patch: A software update that closes a known security hole or vulnerability in a computer program.

phishing: A scam by which email users are duped into revealing personal, confidential, or monetary information or downloading malware by clicking on a malicious link or attachment.

plugins: Applications or programs that can be installed as part of your web browser and allow the program to perform additional tasks.

primary email address: The email address you use for day-to-day purposes.

ransomware: A type of malware used by hackers that encrypts the victim's data and demands payment for the decryption key.

scareware: A type of malware that pretends to be antivirus or antispyware software but tricks people into purchasing or downloading the product and infecting their computer.

security hole: A weakness in a program (software, operating system, etc.) that allows unauthorized access to a system or network.

skimming: A fraud in which identity thieves use a device to capture victims' personal information. They steal information stored in the magnetic strip of credit or bank cards as the victim uses it to make a purchase, and then uses it to make fraudulent purchases.

software: Programs and other operating information used by a computer to perform specific tasks.

spam: Unsolicited, undesired email that is sent to large numbers of people.

spoofed email: The process of creating a fake "from line" in an email to make it appear as though the email came from another source.

Spyware: Malicious software secretly installed on a computer to steal data about its user and transmit the information to a third party.

Trojan horse: A malicious computer program that is used to hack into a computer or device.

two-step verification: A two-stage process to verify your identity when trying to access an online account. It requires "something you know" and "something you have."

viruses: A type of malware that reproduces itself to infect other programs on a computer or device.

virtual private network (VPN): A network technology that creates a private encrypted Internet connection using a public Internet connection.

Wi-Fi: A wireless networking technology that allows computers, smartphones, or other devices to connect to the Internet or communicate with one another wirelessly within a particular area.

> **public Wi-Fi:** A wireless connection that's available to the general public, usually not password-protected.

> **private Wi-Fi:** A wireless connection that's not available to everyone (e.g. the wireless network in your home), usually password-protected.

wireless router: A device that provides wireless Internet access for a home or small office; multiple devices can be connected.

> **Wi-Fi Protected Setup (WPS):** A router setting that makes it easier for devices to connect to the Internet—and also less secure. Users can enter a PIN or push a button to easily connect rather than entering a Wi-Fi password.

> **Wi-Fi Protected Access (WPA/WPA2):** A secure router setting that better encrypts your data. The encryption creates a private tunnel for data to flow though, making it difficult for outsiders to access.

> **Wired Equivalent Privacy (WEP):** An older form of router encryption that is no longer considered secure.

worms: Malware that can replicate itself to spread and infect other computers or devices.

Acknowledgments

Many people had a hand in contributing to *Hack-Proof Your Life Now!* I'm grateful, first and foremost, to Bill T. Nicklin, who supported and encouraged our plans for creating an educational workshop that teaches people how to quickly improve their online security. That effort started with our presentation called "One Hour to Savvy Cybersecurity," led to the Savvy Cybersecurity training program and monthly newsletter by the same name, and finally evolved into this book.

Bill has a tremendous Joe Torre–like leadership style of trust, respect, and optimism that makes working with him at Horsesmouth a pleasure and privilege. He saw what Devin and I saw: people and organizations were vulnerable to a range of cybersecurity threats; advice on how to respond was fragmented and inconsistent; and people needed a framework and guidance for staying safe online. His continued belief in our work helped us reach this point.

This book could not have been written without the steady, dedicated, and energetic support and collaboration of my colleague and coauthor Devin Kropp. Her brilliant EMAIL acronym energized our early research and should help you steer clear of ransomware. Devin always inspires confidence. I'm thankful for all her hard work, her openness to new challenges, and her patience and good cheer through the many zigzags we've made in the last three years.

Many thanks to our project editor, Gail Harrington, who provided gentle yet incisive direction through four manuscript drafts, at all times of day, and over two continents. Her calmness and encouragement kept the project moving forward. Gail embodies the magic of life's chance encounters: I sat down next to her on a rock in Central Park in 1999, amidst 40,000 people. Special shout-out to the Dalai Lama for assisting in our introduction.

My wife and partner in life, Nancy Schwartz, is a rock of strength and a model of good living, whom I learn from all the time. She provided untold hours of support and encouragement, especially during critical writing periods. Nancy was always quick with useful advice and insights.

A special mention of appreciation to the 2,000 financial advisors who assisted our research by answering our survey questions on cybersecurity. Their insights, experiences, and anecdotes about online security challenges helped shape our vision for the Savvy Cybersecurity program and this book.

Debbie Weil offered valuable suggestions as we grappled with how to translate an interactive workshop presentation into a book outline that would be engaging and informative without being depressing and discouraging.

A tip of the hat to Dan Roam, who inspired us to follow his back-of-the-napkin "visual thinking" as we brainstormed concepts for simple illustrations in our Savvy Cybersecurity presentation and now this book. Illustrator Marissa Bernstel expertly translated our Roam-influenced vision into drawings that work.

One author who influenced how we went about creating this book is Sam Horn. We were inspired by her books—especially *Pop!* and *Got Your Attention?*—which do such a great job of engaging and walking readers through a step-by-step process for getting things done.

Sarah Lester and Joanne Beckerich graciously allowed us to present and test our cybersecurity ideas during a couple of presentations at the Maplewood Memorial Library in my hometown of Maplewood, New Jersey. Our library is at the forefront of similar institutions expanding and deepening their missions as centers of learning and community.

Writer and financial consultant Bryan Mills offered thoughtful, enthusiastic insights on cybersecurity, and we appreciate his willingness to test-drive our ideas in public.

Horsesmouth's own Miriam Lawrence, Elaine Floyd, Wendi Webb, and Penny Wolfe were a constant source of help, keeping us abreast of their security observations and feeding us questions about the latest data breach or identity-theft scheme.

We're grateful to those who read parts of the manuscript and offered comments, including Sydney LeBlanc and Frances Bailey.

Brendan Tween and Mark Ursel keep our networks secure at Horsesmouth and answer our tech questions when some detail stumps us. Thanks, and keep it up!

A note of appreciation to our marketing and customer support team, especially Dawn Chamberlain, Melissa Daniel, Cathie Ward, and Cliff Moulton for all their hard work and support over the years at Horsesmouth, and Janet Bernstel for her snappy, compelling videos. Thanks to Doug Pierce who guided us through the creation of our new podcast, *Hack Talk*, and is always a calm presence during our training webinars. Praise to designer Steve Pazenzski for his handiwork on the cover and for the book's website, www.hackproofyourlifenow.com.

We owe a special debt of gratitude to the leading thinkers in the field of cybersecurity whose work informed and inspired our development of the core principles of Savvy Cybersecurity, which grew into the New Cybersecurity Rules. Many experts have issued warnings and shared valuable insights and advice about online security. Chief among them are Graham Cluley, Brian Krebs, and Bruce Schneier.

About the Authors

Sean M. Bailey

Sean is the founding editor in chief of Horsesmouth, a New York-based company that creates educational programs on retirement planning, Social Security, Medicare, college planning, and cybersecurity for industry professionals from top firms including Ameriprise, LPL, Merrill Lynch, Morgan Stanley, Northwestern, Raymond James, UBS, and Wells Fargo. He pioneered computer-assisted reporting in the late 1980s, along with his colleagues at the *News & Observer* of Raleigh, using public-record data to probe government programs. Sean was honored by the North Carolina Press Association for his investigative reporting, covering local politics and white-collar crime. He was an early promoter of the Internet in the 1990s and led a national conference series for the *Philanthropy Journal* teaching nonprofits about technology and online fundraising. Sean launched the Savvy Cybersecurity training program in 2013, an interactive workshop to teach people to boost their security. He lives with his wife and daughter in Maplewood, New Jersey.

Devin Kropp

Devin first experienced the shock associated with identity theft as an 11-year-old in 2002. Just before Christmas, hackers stole her father's debit-card information and sold it to a thief in Spain, who drained several thousand dollars from the account. As a millennial, she's a digital native. She started computer classes in elementary school, received her first PC in the fifth grade, and participated in one of the nation's first e-learning experiments equipping students with laptops. Devin is a graduate of Binghamton University (SUNY) where she studied English and journalism, and played wing and scrum-half for the Women's Rugby Club. She joined Horsesmouth in 2013 as an associate editor. Devin lives in Manhattan.

We Want to Hear from You!

It's our mission to boost everyone's cybersecurity.

We invite you to stay in touch and join our informal network of Hack-Proof contributors. Do you have any stories about cyber crime, web scams, or identity theft? The more people know about an active, effective cyber fraud, the quicker it can be shut down and people alerted. We're collecting tips, insights, and anecdotes about people's experiences with the latest online security scams. We'll keep your name private, of course, but investigate and report back to our followers on Facebook, Twitter, LinkedIn and YouTube. Naturally, we'll issue warnings and guidelines about new threats, too.

Want to arrange for Sean and Devin to teach the New Cyber-security Rules to your conference, organization, or company? Their Savvy Cybersecurity program is a fun, engaging, and interactive presentation that will quickly boost an audience's online security and set them up to stay secure. Want to train professionals in your firm or association to spot malware, avoid identity theft, and foil hackers? Sean and Devin will teach professionals to present their Hack-Proof ideas to colleagues, community organizations, schools, and any group in need of cybersecurity guidance.

Sean and Devin are also available for radio, podcast, TV, blog, newspaper, or magazine interviews. They can talk about the latest cybersecurity news and connect the headlines with the core principles of smart, effective cybersecurity.

We're constantly abreast of the latest online security developments. Stay in touch by following our blog at www.hackproofyourlifenow.com. Connect with us on Facebook at Hack-Proof Your Life Now!, and Twitter @hackproofadvice. You can also find us on LinkedIn and YouTube. Listen to our podcast *Hack Talk*, which you can find on iTunes, SoundCloud, and Stitcher.

If you're interested in buying copies of *Hack-Proof Your Life Now!* we can provide you with a number of options for customization and bulk purchase discounts.

Contact us by email at hackproof@horsesmouth.com or call us at the Horsesmouth headquarters in Manhattan: 888-336-6884 or 212-343-8760.

Horsesmouth

Horsesmouth is an independent publisher and training company that educates professionals and the general public about the increasingly complex decisions that shape our financial lives, including: *How do we get the best financial aid package for college? How do I protect my family from hackers? How do we coordinate our retirement plans? When should we take Social Security? What health care options and Medicare plans make sense for us?*

Financial professionals turn to our Savvy Series for resources to teach the public and guide clients through these critical decisions. Savvy programs provide year-round educational materials, tools, and ongoing support. They also include communication programs to help professionals become the go-to resource in their communities. The series includes Savvy Social Security Planning® (savvysocialsecurity .com), Savvy Medicare Planning℠ (savvymedicare.net), Savvy IRA Planning® (savvyira.com), Savvy College Planning℠ (savvycollegeplanning.com), and Savvy Cybersecurity™ (savvycybersecurity.com).

Horsesmouth, founded in 1996, is headquartered in Manhattan, with employees across the country.

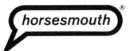

21 West 38th Street, 14th Floor, New York, NY 10018
Voice: (888) 33-Mouth (888-336-6884)
Fax: (212) 363-9526
www.horsesmouth.com
sales@horsesmouth.com

Index

annual credit report monitoring, 185

Do Not Call list, 184

Do Not Mail list, 184

identity theft protection services, reasons not recommended, 123–125

lost or stolen wallet protection, 184

reduce pre-approved credit card offers, 184

security freeze, 123, 124–125

psychology of security, 58–61

financial omniscience, 60–61

irrational security trade-offs, 60

optimism bias, 58

reacting to risk, two systems, 60

risk and reward duel, 59–60

Q

quiz, discover your Cybersecurity Score, 5–7

R

ransomware extortion, 102–106

eFax spam mail, 2–3

hack report, 103–104

paying ransom, 180–181

bitcoins, 180–181

differing opinions on whether to pay, 104

no backup, need to pay, 106

statistics, number of victims and amount of ransom paid, 105

ransomware programs, 104–105

what to do if you get infected, 106

Reaper, first antivirus software program, 90–91

recycled passwords, 32

hack report, 31

restart computer

"restart your computer" myth, 99

restarting computer

postponing restart, 177–178

risk and the psychology of security

reacting to risk, 60

risk and reward duel, 59–60

router information, identifying, 145–146

manufacturer, 145

model number, 145

router's IP address, 145–146

routers, home Wi-Fi networks, 42–43, 147–150

change router username and password, 42, 43, 147

disable WPS, 42, 43, 147–148

encrypt your router, 42, 43, 147

firmware, updating, 43, 148–149

hack report, 41–42

"rule of three," 105–106

S

Safari, phishing detection features, 183

Safe Mode

Malwarebytes program, 169

Samsung. *See* Android devices

scareware

"fake antivirus scam," 92

virus scam, 89–90

Schneier, Bruce, 58–60

Scientific American, 15

secret email account for financial/bank accounts, set up guidelines, 19, 136–137

email address, 136

login, two-step protection, 138

password reset, 136–137

reduce your digital footprint, 19

strong password creation. *See* password strengthening

Secunia report, 177

security freeze on credit files, 70–71, 157–159

children. *See* security freeze on credit files for children

fees, 158

lifting or removing the freeze, 158

placing freeze on credit files, 157–158

online, 157

telephone, 157

protection against identity theft, 123, 124–125